WEST GERMANY
On the Road to Reunification

PLACES AND PEOPLES OF THE WORLD

WEST GERMANY

On the Road to Reunification

Sean Dolan

CHELSEA HOUSE PUBLISHERS
New York Philadelphia

COVER: Looking out over the Alpsee in Bavaria, is Hohenschwangau Castle (center), built in the 1830s. Standing over the gorge, at the top right with its pinnacles and towers, is Neuschwanstein Castle, constructed in 1869.
FRONTISPIECE: The 1897 Rathaus (city hall) of Hamburg dominates the town square with its tall campanile.

Chelsea House Publishers
Editor-in-Chief: Remmel Nunn
Managing Editor: Karyn Gullen Browne
Copy Chief: Juliann Barbato
Picture Editor: Adrian G. Allen
Art Director: Maria Epes
Deputy Copy Chief: Mark Rifkin
Assistant Art Director: Noreen Romano
Manufacturing Manager: Gerald Levine
Systems Manager: Lindsey Ottman
Production Manager: Joseph Romano
Production Coordinator: Marie Claire Cebrián

Places and Peoples of the World
Senior Editor: Kathy Kuhtz

Staff for WEST GERMANY
Copy Editor: Karen Hammonds
Picture Researcher: Lisa Kirchner
Designer: Debora Smith

First Printing
1 3 5 7 9 8 6 4 2

Library of Congress Cataloging-in-Publication Data
Dolan, Sean.
West Germany: On the Road to Reunification/Sean Dolan.
p. cm.—(Places and peoples of the world)
Includes index.
Summary: An introduction to the geography, history, government, economy, people, and culture of West Germany.
ISBN 0-7910-1367-7
1. Germany (West)—Juvenile literature. [1. Germany (West)]
I. Title. II. Series.
DD258.3.D65 1990 90-2307
943—dc20 CIP AC

CONTENTS

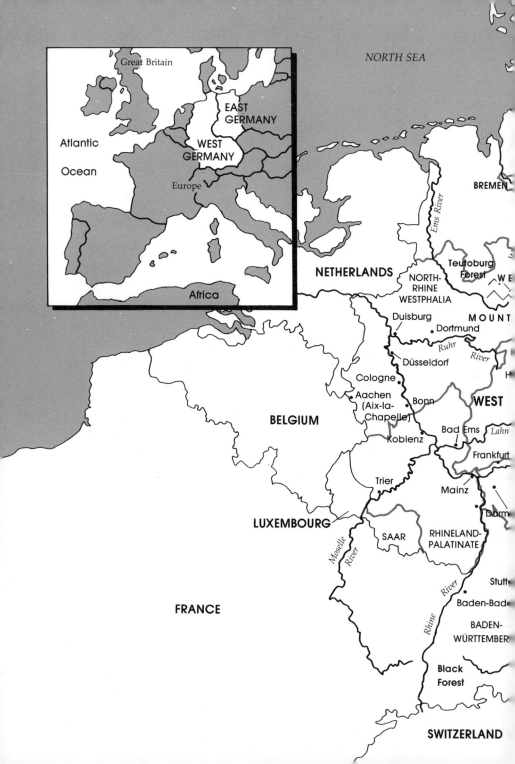

FACTS AT A GLANCE

Land and People

Official Name Federal Republic of Germany

Capital Bonn (population 286,000)

Other Major Cities West Berlin (population 2 million); Hamburg (population 1.7 million); Munich (population 1.3 million); Cologne (population 1 million); Frankfurt (population 625,000); Stuttgart (population 550,000); and Bremen (population 550,000)

Language German

Population 62 million (approximately)

Area 95,929 square miles (248,454 square kilometers)

Density 630 per square mile (243 per square kilometer)

Distribution 75 percent of the population live in urban areas

Armed Forces 550,000; largest in Western Europe

Religion In 1990, 96 percent of the West German people professed membership in a church; Roman Catholicism and Protestantism each claimed about 50 percent of that number

Infant Mortality Rate	7 per 1,000 live births
Average Life Expectancy	72 years for men, 79 years for women
Literacy Rate	99 percent
Holidays	Easter, Pentecost, Christmas, June 2 (Proclamation of the Republic Day), Oktoberfest
Highest Point	The Zugspitze, 9,721 feet (2,963 meters)
Mountain Ranges	Bavarian Alps, Swabian Jura, Weser Mountains, and Harz Mountains
Rivers	Danube, Rhine, Elbe, Main, Moselle, and Oder
Climate	Temperate maritime

Economy

Currency	Deutsche mark (DM), divided into 100 pfennigs; U.S. $1 equal to approximately 1.64 DM in 1990
Per Capita Gross National Product	$11,730 (U.S. dollars)
Chief Agricultural Products	Wheat, barley, potatoes, beets, pork, beer, and wine
Major Industries	Manufacturing, especially automobiles, farm and electrical equipment, iron and steel, chemicals, heavy machinery and industrial equipment, services, commerce, and banking
Natural Resources	Iron ore, coal, natural gas, and petroleum
Energy	Oil, much of it imported, supplied more than half of West Germany's energy needs
Transportation	More than 20,000 miles of railroad system, 90 percent of it government-owned; more than 4,000 miles of *autobahn* (high-speed highway) system; extensive mass transit systems, particularly in urban areas; most major cities accessible by air

Government

Form	Constitutional democracy
Law of the Land	The constitution, known as the Basic Law
Legislative Assembly	Consisted of two chambers, the Bundestag and the Bundesrat
Head of Government	The chancellor, who was head of the party maintaining a working majority in the Bundestag
Head of State	The president, chosen by popular election
Major Political Parties	Christian Democratic Union and Social Democratic party
Political Divisions	10 *Länder*, or states, plus West Berlin

HISTORY AT A GLANCE

1356 Golden Bull formalizes the procedure for electing the Holy Roman Emperor.

ca. 1400 Extensive eastward migration of German-speaking people begins.

1438 Albert II is crowned Holy Roman Emperor; he is the first Habsburg emperor of the dynasty that will rule until 1806.

1455 Johannes Gutenberg develops the first printing press.

1528 The death of Albrecht Dürer, the great German painter, printmaker, and theoretician.

1618–48 The Thirty Years' War rages in Germany.

1701 Friedrich I is crowned king of Prussia.

1740–63 Friedrich II, or Frederick the Great, leads Prussia to victory in the War of the Austrian Succession and the Seven Years' War.

1774 Johann Wolfgang von Goethe's *The Sorrows of Young Werther* is published.

1806 Napoléon Bonaparte invades Germany and abolishes the Holy Roman Empire.

1815 Diplomats at the Congress of Vienna establish the Confederation of Germany, thereby ensuring continued German political fragmentation.

1827 Composer Ludwig van Beethoven dies.

1862 Kaiser Wilhelm I appoints Otto von Bismarck chancellor of Prussia.

1866 Prussia defeats Austria in the Austro-Prussian War.

1870–71 Bismarck goads France into war; Prussia's victory leads to formation of a unified German state under Prussian leadership.

1890 Kaiser Wilhelm II dismisses Bismarck; Bismarck dies in 1898.

1914–18   World War I is fought; Germany is defeated.

1919–33   The postwar Weimar Republic governs; it is a period of ruinous economic troubles in Germany; Expressionism movement reaches its peak.

1933   Adolf Hitler becomes chancellor of Germany and quickly assumes dictatorial powers.

1933–45   Hitler imprisons and kills millions of European Jews; Germany is defeated in World War II.

1949   Creation of the Federal Republic of Germany as a capitalist, Western-oriented, democratic nation.

1949–63   Konrad Adenauer governs as chancellor, presiding over the period of the West German economic miracle.

1971   Chancellor Willy Brandt wins the Nobel Peace Prize for the policy of reconciliation with East Germany.

1990   Rapid political changes in Eastern Europe bring West and East Germany to the brink of reunification: on July 1, economic and currency union begins, and Soviet president Mikhail Gorbachev and West German chancellor Helmut Kohl agree on the membership of a united Germany in the North Atlantic Treaty Organization (NATO). On October 2, France, England, and the United States cede their status as occupying powers to the unified German state after 45 years of authority, and on October 3, West Germany and East Germany reunite, becoming the Federal Republic of Germany. On October 14, state elections are held in East Germany, followed by the first parliamentary elections including both Germanys on December 2.

In June 1990, Prime Minister Lothar de Maizière (foreground) of East Germany and Chancellor Helmut Kohl (background) of West Germany leave a conference in Bonn. With political reunification of the two Germanys imminent, the two leaders were preparing for Germany's rise to the status of economic superpower.

1

West Germany and the World

Over a matter of months at the close of the 1980s, it seemed that the entire order of things in Eastern Europe—often depicted in the Western media as a joyless region of government-enforced poverty, grim conformity, economic mismanagement, and lockstep compliance with the dictates of the Soviet Union—had unraveled. Since the end of World War II in 1945, Eastern Europe had been seen by the West as a Communist monolith, its ideological enemy in the political and economic struggle for worldwide influence known as the *cold war*. Suddenly, in a stunningly short period of time, under the impetus of a program of reform and restructuring set in motion by the premier of the Soviet Union, Mikhail Gorbachev, and the force of the long pent-up hopes and dreams of Eastern Europeans, all that seemed to change.

Perhaps most amazing were the changes in Germany, the nation whose division into two nations—one a democratic republic, the other a one-party Communist dictatorship—in the late 1940s had come to symbolize the greater division of Europe. For it was in

Germany that the presence of a physical divider—the Berlin Wall—across its former capital city had come to symbolize the many, seemingly permanent barriers between East and West in the postwar era that the former British prime minister Winston Churchill had called in 1948 the Iron Curtain. Faced with a renewed migration to its western counterpart that rivaled the great exodus of the immediate postwar years, East Germany announced in 1989 that it was loosening and then lifting the severe restrictions on travel to the West that for years had held many of its reluctant citizens virtually captive.

What followed were scenes of unparalleled jubilation, as tens of thousands of East Germans, by car and on foot, swarmed across the border, some to stay, some to shop, some to celebrate, some to simply look around. Families divided for more than 40 years were tearfully reunited. In Berlin, formerly stone-faced East German border guards smiled and drank beer with revelers and tourists as ecstatic Berliners took jackhammers and sledgehammers to the

On November 10, 1989, East Germans help each other climb the Berlin Wall as they celebrate the opening of the East German borders near the Brandenburg Gate. Eastern authorities had erected the wall of concrete and barbed wire across the heart of the former capital city in 1961 to halt the flow of refugees into West Berlin.

Wall. In the euphoria, Germans began to express hope—hesitantly at first, as if they did not dare to express the thought, then increasingly boldly and confidently—that the easing of tensions between the two Germanys would culminate in reunification. Events in Germany rushed headlong in that direction, leading to the free elections in East Germany in March 1990 that resulted in the defeat of the Communists and the election of the Alliance of Germany, a conservative coalition favoring reunification and closely allied with West Germany's governing party, the Christian Democratic Union (CDU). A new note of sobriety became evident in discussions of the cavalcade of events in Eastern Europe, a tone very much at odds with the elation that characterized so much of the immediately preceding period.

Perhaps things have moved just a little bit too swiftly, was the gist of this new message; perhaps a cooling-off period, a time for reflection on the meaning of all these changes, would be prudent. Others, among them prominent Germans such as the internationally acclaimed novelist Günter Grass, were more blunt. Germany should not be reunited, said Grass, author of such imaginative, symbolic examinations of German culture and history as *The Tin Drum* and *Dog Years*. If to some the monumental changes in Germany and the rest of Europe at the end of the 1980s represented a long-awaited end to the myriad horrors brought about by World War II, others suggested that the best course of action was remembrance, not forgetting. According to Michel Debre, the former prime minister of France, the prospect of German reunification should have been the occasion for profound German consternation, not celebration: "We French, who know our neighbors well, how can we not remind all Europeans and the world as a whole of the need to guard against abuses which Germany commits in all areas when it sees an opportunity?" Fritz Stern, a professor of history at Columbia University in New York City, put it more succinctly. "The Germans want to think of the future," he said, "but their neighbors are thinking of the past." Once again, the German question has become the most crucial issue of the day for Europe.

Its Problematical Endowment

Germany has long been a mystery and a torment, both to its neighbors and to itself. "The Germans are the really problematical people," wrote Thomas Mann, in all likelihood the greatest of German novelists, author of *Buddenbrooks, Death in Venice, The Magic Mountain, Doctor Faustus,* and *The Beloved Returns* and winner of the Nobel Prize in literature in 1929. Mann went on to say that "Whosoever should strive to transform Germany . . . would be trying to rob her of her best and weightiest quality, of her problematical endowment, which is the essence of her nationality."

Nor was Mann the first or the only German literary figure to comment on the singular character and qualities of his countrymen. The question of national and personal identity has been a dominant theme in German literature, perhaps because of all the great European powers, Germany was the last to become a unified nation. Johann Wolfgang von Goethe, whose poems, plays, and novels made him a towering figure of the Romantic period (1790–1850), believed that "the Germans make everything difficult, both for themselves and for everyone else." It is appropriate that this study of West Germany begin with quotations from two of Germany's greatest authors, for few nations can boast of a prouder literary or cultural legacy. It was the Romantic philosopher and writer Johann Gottfried von Herder who suggested that one might best begin with a country's literature if one wishes to understand that nation: "Has a nation anything more precious? From a study of native literature we have learned to know ages and peoples more deeply than along the sad and frustrating path of political and military history. In the latter we seldom see more than the

Johann Wolfgang von Goethe (1749–1832), poet, dramatist, novelist, and scientist, is considered by many to be the most important German writer. Goethe was a compassionate and vulnerable individual who grappled with a variety of human crises during the great social and intellectual revolutions of the late 18th century and left a crucial record of his myriad experiences.

manner in which a people was ruled, how it let itself be slaughtered; in the former we learn how it thought, what it wished and craved for, how it took its pleasures, how it was led by its teachers or its inclinations."

Nor is Germany's cultural achievement confined to poetry and fiction. The paintings of Albrecht Dürer, Lucas Cranach the Elder, Hans Holbein the Younger, and Matthias Grünewald remain among the highest embodiments of medieval and Renaissance art. The philosophical treatises of such thinkers as Gottfried Wilhelm Leibniz, Immanuel Kant, Johann Gottlieb Fichte, and Georg Wilhelm Friedrich Hegel changed the course of Western thought, and the world would be a much poorer place without the beautiful symphonies, concertos, oratorios, operas, and other works of such revered German composers as Ludwig van Beethoven, Johannes Brahms, Johann Sebastian Bach, Richard Wagner, and Robert Schumann.

What then, in Mann's view, is problematic about the German people, and why is it important? How then, in consideration of

Goethe's thesis, do the Germans make things difficult for themselves and others? Why then, does such an undercurrent of trepidation attend talk about German reunification? Despite Herder's disclaimer, German history helps provide an immediate answer. Between 1740 and 1763, the forces of the German state of Prussia, commanded by the enlightened despot Friedrich II, called Frederick the Great, twice overran most of the central and eastern part of the continent. During the War of the Austrian Succession (1740–48) and the Seven Years' War (1756–63), Friedrich II's troops occupied much of present-day Czechoslovakia, Hungary, Poland, and Romania. Bloodshed and destruction accompanied the Prussian troops as they made their conquests. In both cases, it was German aggression that sparked the wars. A highly cultured person who was ahead of his time in implementing progressive social legislation in his kingdom, Friedrich II played the flute and wrote music and poetry, but he was also a cunning military strategist who could be ruthless in battle. "Dogs! Would you live forever?" he was said to shout at those Prussian infantrymen slow to throw themselves to the fore during combat. The reign of Friedrich II launched Germany's enduring reputation for militarism and unwarranted aggression.

A little more than 100 years after the close of the Seven Years' War, Prussia turned its sights westward and invaded the neighboring nation of France. Victory was swift—the French capital of Paris fell in January 1871, about five months after the war began—and resulted in the formation of the German Empire. France was forced to relinquish its provinces of Alsace and Lorraine to the newly united Germany.

But Germany's greatest transgressions came in the 20th century. When Germany backed Austria-Hungary in its declaration of war against the Balkan nation of Serbia (now part of Yugoslavia) in the summer of 1914, it helped unleash a conflagration that devastated most of Europe. When German forces invaded France, Belgium, and Russia, the casualties on both sides reached catastrophic proportions. By the time World War I ended in November 1918, an estimated 10 million Europeans and Americans had been killed. More than twice that number had been wounded, and the economic and spiritual damage to the European continent was simply impossible to estimate.

At war's end the European nations met, as they had done several times in the past, to consider measures that would rein in or neutralize Germany. But the heavy reparations and harsh economic strictures mandated by the Treaty of Versailles proved insufficient to prevent a resurgent German nation from rearming and terrorizing Europe once again. Preying on racial fears, economic disturbances, and German resentment at being made the scapegoats for World War I, Adolf Hitler was named chancellor of Germany in 1933. He quickly assumed dictatorial powers, crushed all opposition, and embarked on a program of conquest and territorial expansion. In 1938 he annexed Austria and bullied the European powers into awarding him a portion of Czechoslovakia; his invasion of Poland in September of the following year began World War II. Just 21 years after the "war to end all wars" concluded, the world was again convulsed in violent conflict. Hitler's plan to establish a Third German *Reich* (empire or kingdom) included his so-called Final Solution: the extermination of all of Europe's Jews, whom he believed to be responsible for Germany's economic woes and to be a racially inferior taint on Germany's pure Aryan stock. It took six years of fighting and the combined military might of the United States, Great Britain, France, and the Soviet Union to subdue Hitler's Germany. By that time a good portion of Europe had again been reduced to rubble, and 6 million Jews, among others, had been put to death in Hitler's concentration camps.

The tradition of militarism, especially when it was taken to the extreme by Hitler, makes it easy to see why observers, literary and otherwise, have speculated about the problematic aspects of the German national character. Although not denying the majesty of Germany's cultural achievement, litterateurs, historians, psychologists, and others have suggested that the country's excesses in war have been the product not merely of historical and economic forces but reflect as well fundamental aspects of the German character. The well-known German love of order, the characteristic German respect for authority, and the culturally bred conformity of German society has made Germans susceptible to governmental authoritarianism and unlikely to protest when their government exceeds the bounds of constitutional behavior, states this argument. Indeed, some hold that Germans worship power and might and that this affinity has manifested itself throughout history in the glorification of the military and the power of the state.

In the years following the *Stunde Null*, or zero hour, in 1945, when the German people awoke to discover their government toppled, their cities bombed into vast junk heaps and mounds of debris, their economy shattered, their land occupied by four foreign victors, and themselves regarded as morally contemptible by the world, the question of national identity has taken on increased significance. Until recently Germany was divided into two separate nations politically and physically, as it had been since 1949. East Germany, known officially as the German Democratic Republic, was until March 1990 governed by a Communist regime and was closely allied with the Soviet Union. And on October 3, 1990, East Germany essentially ceased to exist, reuniting with the Federal Republic of Germany, or West Germany, taking on its name, anthem, constitution, and way of government. The subject of this book, West Germany, was governed by a democratically elected chancellor and parliament and was one of the most valued and strategically important allies of the United States. Its economic recovery from the ravages of its most recent war was little short of miraculous; along with Japan, another defeated aggressor in World War II, West Germany prior to unification boasted one of the world's most prosperous economies and highest standards of living. German engineering has made its luxury and sports cars—Porsches, Mercedes-Benzes, and BMWs—prized by drivers around the world, while fuel- and cost-conscious motorists continue to buy Volkswagens in large numbers. The *rapprochement* (reconciliation) between West German industry and the country's labor unions made it the envy of other nations bedeviled by labor woes. Even before reunification became a viable possibility, Europeans worried that West Germany was destined to dominate the European Community, as the proposed European common market is to be known. The addition of the productive capacity of East Germany, the most prosperous nation in the Eastern bloc, will in all likelihood make West Germany's economic power that much greater. West Germany's economic success has led to resentment by the peoples of other nations, who wonder if perhaps Germany was treated too leniently following World War II and question whether the Germans have ever learned the proper lesson from their history. It is a question that many Germans ask themselves as well. With the two Germanys reunited as one nation, but with many questions remaining as to the specifics of how this is to be accomplished, the German preoccupation with personal and national identity persists largely unsettled. That obsession may best be understood by examining the historical events that have shaped the nation and its people. Upon reunification, in the eyes of most outside observers and the Germans themselves, the 41-year history of West Germany thus becomes an extremely brief chapter in a much longer and more important story—the ongoing struggle of all of Germany to define itself as a nation.

In Rome, Pope Leo III crowns Charlemagne emperor on Christmas Day in 800. As emperor, Charlemagne—who was a champion of Christianity—assumed jurisdiction over the Roman Empire, set up an efficient administrative system by which to rule his empire, and had the law of his domain codified.

2

Like None but Themselves

Literary observation of the unique character of the Germans began early. Writing in the first century A.D., the distinguished Roman historian Tacitus, whose *Germania* recounted the failed attempts of the legions of the Roman Empire to subdue the bellicose inhabitants of the land between the Rhine and Oder rivers, defined the Germans as a "distinct, unmixed race, like none but themselves." Several decades earlier, warriors of this singular people had ambushed and defeated a proud, battle-tested force of 20,000 Roman soldiers that made the mistake of leaving the main military highway and venturing into the thick Teutoburger Wald, or Teutoburg Forest (in the present-day *Land*, or state, of North Rhine–Westphalia). Only a handful of the Romans survived to fight another day; the rest were killed in battle, enslaved, tortured to death, or sacrificed to the local gods. Tacitus called the battle frenzy exhibited by the Germans the *furor Teutonicus* (the word *Teutonic* is used to refer to the Germanic peoples) and observed that the Germans were "fanatically loyal to their leaders." Their stamina seemed boundless; according to Tacitus, "Rest is unwelcome to the race." Soon after the Battle of Teutoburger Wald, all

the Roman outposts east of the Rhine River save one—Aliso—
were overrun. The fortunate defenders of Aliso fled back across
the Rhine, and with their retreat serious Roman attempts to sub-
jugate the land it called *Germania barbaria* (barbarian Germany)
essentially ended. The Rhine and the Danube rivers, connected
by a 300-mile line of fortifications known as the *limes*, came to
mark the borders of the Roman Empire, and the fierce Germanic
tribes were left to themselves, for the time being.

Barbarians at the Gate

As the Roman Empire weakened under the force of internal and
external pressures, the Germanic tribes filled the vacuum left by
its demise. Among these were the Franks, the Visigoths, the
Ostrogoths, the Lombards, and the Saxons. These barbarians, as
the Romans referred to them—the word was used in the ancient
world to refer to any non-Roman people—nipped at the flanks of
the empire in the east and the west. By the early years of the 5th
century, they threatened the city of Rome itself: It was sacked by
the Visigoth king Alaric in 410 and by another barbarian leader,
Gaiseric, in 455. The German tribes had yet to develop a sense of
national identity, however, and they remained divided, unable to
fill the void left by the fall of the Roman Empire in the west.

The Carolingian Empire

The Franks eventually emerged as the most powerful German
tribe, conquering their rivals and establishing control over ter-
ritories that stretched from the Pyrenees in the west (the present-
day border between Spain and France) to the Oder River in the
east, a region that encompassed most of modern France, Germany,
the Netherlands, and Belgium as well as a portion of northern
Italy. The greatest Frankish king, Karl der Große, known as Charlemagne or Charles the Great, assumed the throne in 768. During
his reign, the Carolingian Empire reached its largest extent, and
he was instrumental in spreading Christianity among the other

Germanic peoples, such as the conquered Saxons. On Christmas Day in 800, in recognition of his services to a papacy beleaguered by challenges to its authority, Pope Leo III crowned Charlemagne emperor.

The Holy Roman Empire

The coronation of Charlemagne was intended to symbolize the rebirth of the Roman Empire. At its peak, the Roman Empire had extended throughout most of the region along the Mediterranean Sea, into the Middle East and North Africa, and had also included Spain, France (which the Romans called Gaul), and even England. Few of these dominions had failed to be profoundly influenced by Roman civilization and most had benefited, not least through the sense of order that Rome imposed on a tumultuous world. Those subjects who agreed to the *Pax Romana*—the terms of peace that Rome imposed upon its conquered enemies—could at least rest secure in the knowledge that Roman might was pledged to protect them against whatever enemies threatened. Although Rome was always first and foremost a military power, its vassal states could count on enjoying a degree of peace and self-government largely unknown outside the empire, so long as they provided the tribute that Rome demanded.

After the fall of Rome, no power existed that could provide the same sense of order and security in Europe. The term sometimes used to describe the roughly 1,000 years that began with Rome's fall—the Dark Ages—reflects the feeling that Europe then entered a period of decline. In Rome's absence, Christianity became the closest thing to a unifying force. By the time of Charlemagne's coronation, virtually all of Europe had been converted, but just as Rome had been beleaguered by the barbarians, Christianity was challenged by the spread of Islam, the religion established by the prophet Mohammed on the Arabian Peninsula in the 6th century. Islam had spread quickly throughout the Middle East and Africa, and in the 8th century the Moors, North African Muslims, had carried it into Spain. Its advance was halted in 732 at the Battle of Tours, in France, where Charlemagne's grandfather, Charles Martel (Charles the Hammer) defeated a large Moorish force, but in Charlemagne's day it remained firmly established in Spain and also menaced Christian Europe from the east, where it had made inroads on the Balkan Peninsula.

Although most popes of the Middle Ages were of necessity worldly figures very like any of Europe's princes and kings, Christianity was a religious, not a political, doctrine, and the popes exercised their greatest authority in spiritual matters. Because religion was of paramount importance during the Middle Ages and affected virtually every aspect of daily life, this spiritual authority cannot be overestimated. Nevertheless, the popes also saw Christianity as the divinely ordained successor to the Roman Empire and themselves as the head of that empire. They also recognized that their ability to exercise the temporal (worldly, as opposed to spiritual) power to which they aspired was to a large extent dependent upon their ability to maintain the support of the princes and kings who possessed the power to do such extremely useful things as gather funds through taxation and, most important of all, muster armies. It was also clear to the popes that their ability to defend Christianity against such threats as Islam depended upon good relations with the rulers who could put armies in the field.

The coronation of Charlemagne and his later successors thus represented Rome's (in this sense, Rome as the seat of the papacy, not the Roman Empire) attempt to ally itself with what was then the most powerful state in Europe, the Frankish kingdom. Over time this kingdom would give way to the myriad German states loosely united by their nominal fealty to the Roman-coronated emperor, who was often referred to as the *rex Germanorum* (king of the Germans). This union was intended to be mutually beneficial.

Charlemagne's throne sits in the gallery of his palatine chapel at Aachen (Aix-la-Chapelle). Charlemagne's court at Aachen became a center for an artistic and intellectual renaissance—even his octagonal chapel resembles Roman and Byzantine architecture in its design and decoration.

The papacy, the supreme spiritual head of Christianity, thereby availed itself of the military and temporal power of the emperor, who theoretically became, as the great English historian Lord Bryce stated in *The Holy Roman Empire* (published in 1864), the "viceroy of God" and, as one of his titles officially proclaimed, "the Temporal Head of the Faithful." In accepting the crown from the pope, the emperor ostensibly received the sanction of heaven itself for his reign, providing him with legitimacy that could be challenged only at supreme spiritual peril to the challenger. Over time, this singular arrangement between Rome and the German ruler gave rise to the title Holy Roman Empire of the German Nation to describe the German states.

Church vs. State

In practice, the alliance between Rome and the Holy Roman Emperor was an uneasy one, and the countless machinations and intrigues engaged in by the emperors in their unending struggle with the Roman Catholic church helped inspire Voltaire's famous quip that the empire was neither holy, Roman, nor an empire.

The seeds of future discontent were sown early. Charlemagne arranged for his kingdom to be partitioned among his three sons, none of whom was to be crowned emperor. Over the course of the 9th century, the Frankish kingdom came under constant attack from Viking raiders in the north, Saracen marauders from the south, and Magyar horsemen from the east. Weakened even further by quarrels over succession to the throne, the kingdom ultimately broke apart, with the eastern portion, in particular the duchies of Lorraine, Swabia, Bavaria, Saxony, and Franconia, forming the foundation of what would become modern Germany.

Otto I, a Saxon whose achievements would earn him the sobriquet of "the Great," took the throne in 936 and was crowned Holy Roman Emperor in 962. He halted the Magyar advance and decisively defeated the Slavs, thereby adding what was to become Mecklenburg and Brandenburg to the empire and extending its eastern frontier to the Oder River. In 962, Otto responded to the entreaties of Pope John XII, whose unparalleled licentiousness had inspired his enemies to depose him; Otto marched on Rome and restored John to the Holy See. In return, he received concessions from the pope regarding the emperor's control over the church's administration. Almost immediately following Otto's return to Germany, John renounced his promises and allied himself with

Otto's enemies. Otto returned to Rome and summoned a council to depose John, who went into exile. But when the emperor left once more, John regained his authority and wreaked a terrible vengeance upon his opponents. The tradition of struggle between the Holy Roman Emperor (as the secular authority) and the papacy (as the spiritual authority) had been established.

This conflict reached its climax in the 11th century with the battle between the German emperor Heinrich IV and Pope Gregory VII. Gregory, a Benedictine monk who before his election as pope in 1073 had been called Hildebrand, was the leader of a reform movement in the Catholic church that sought to put an end to such practices as the marriage of clergymen, the selling of church offices, and lay *investiture*. (Investiture meant the appointing of bishops and other high church officials.) German princes had long claimed this prerogative for themselves, and Heinrich IV had no intention of surrendering it to the church. The issue involved more than the filling of church offices, for in Germany appointment to a bishopric brought with it a great deal of temporal power as well as spiritual responsibilities. Church officeholders were in essence the administrators for the kingdom, and bishops, for example, were often responsible for collecting taxes and other revenues as well as for the control of the vast church properties. In the words of historian Donald S. Detwiler, the German bishops were not just clergymen but "leading princes of the empire who directly controlled territorial principalities on a level—in terms of political, economic, and military resources—with the most powerful and important German duchies." It is therefore easy to see why the emperor would wish to control who received these appointments, for it was a means by which he could make some of the most influential officials of the realm beholden to him. If the emperor controlled the bishoprics and by extension the thousands of acres of lucrative church lands, he could use his power of patronage to buy, in essence, the loyalty of the princes, dukes, and margraves—the German nobility—who were constantly seeking to extend their privileges at the expense of the monarchy. What made this power doubly attractive was that at the death of a bishop, for example, the lands that he controlled would not be inherited by his heir, as would be the case with noble property, but would revert to the power—church or emperor—invested with the right to dispense them.

Momentum in this struggle was on the side of the church, which in 1059 had succeeded in eliminating the leading role of the emperor in selecting the pope. It should be noted that at this point Germany was still in no sense a formally unified political state but instead a loose collection of entities, united only through the personal influence of the emperor and a vague, inchoate sense of German nationality. The nobility's greatest loyalty was regional, and it was traditionally concerned not so much with some concept of fidelity to a greater German nation as with the protection of its hereditary rights and privileges within the countless duchies, principalities, palatinates, and other political arrangements into which Germany was carved. Heinrich IV therefore regarded the investiture issue as essential, for he recognized that he needed control over the church offices as a bulwark against the power of the nobility.

When Gregory proved unyielding, Heinrich denounced him, questioning his legitimacy as first father of the church and proclaiming him to be not Gregory, the pope, but Hildebrand, a false monk. Declaring that his rights as emperor were invested in him directly by God, not the pope, Heinrich IV challenged Gregory to relinquish the throne of St. Peter—"Come down, come down, and be damned through all the ages!"

Gregory promptly excommunicated Heinrich IV, an action that held considerably more significance than excluding him from the sacraments of the church, for it meant that in the eyes of Rome,

Heinrich IV no longer possessed authority as the Holy Roman Emperor and that his subjects were in no way obligated to fulfill their vows of loyalty to him. The excommunication was tantamount to announcing that Heinrich had been deposed, and the German nobility had no problem in recognizing it as such. Some nobles were moved by opportunism, others by sincere religious motivation, but many saw a chance to diminish the power of the emperor, and rebellion broke out across Germany.

Wasting no time, Gregory set out for Germany to preside over the election of a new emperor. In 1077 a chastened Heinrich IV intercepted him at Canossa, on the northern slopes of the Apen-

In 1077, Heinrich IV appears barefoot in the snow at Canossa to ask for Pope Gregory VII's forgiveness after his excommunication from the church. Although the power struggle between the Holy Roman Emperor and the pope had its roots in the previous century, Heinrich IV and Gregory VII's fight over who would fill bishoprics became the climax of the conflict.

nines; he then knelt barefoot in the snow for three days outside the pope's castle in humble suppliance for the Holy Father's forgiveness. Gregory, a genuinely spiritual man who was later canonized, did not refuse Heinrich IV absolution, but the German nobles were less compassionate and went right ahead with their plan to elect a new, presumably more compliant, king. Years of civil war ensued, to the detriment of the imperial power. In 1122, at Worms, the city where in 1076 Heinrich IV had forced the German bishops to denounce Gregory VII as a false monk, his son and successor, Heinrich V, conceded the right of investiture to the church, retaining only the symbolic power to be present at the investiture ceremony. More important was the change in the balance of power between the king and the nobility, with the nobility gaining at the monarch's expense. The nobles had elected Germany's kings long before Heinrich IV's dispute with Gregory but in doing so had generally observed the principle of hereditary succession. By acting to depose Heinrich IV, Gregory had rejected the notion that any one family ruled by divine right, thereby encouraging the nobles in their growing independence. From that point onward, the nobles would grow ever more zealous in defending their prerogatives and would come to treat the king, in Detwiler's view, as no better than *primus inter pares*—first among equals.

The Two Friedrichs

Following the death of Heinrich V, the division among the German nobility grew more pronounced, and Germany was racked by civil war. The two predominant parties were the Saxons and Bavarians, known jointly as the Guelphs (the word is derived from the Italian translation of the name of one of the leading Bavarian families, the Welfs), who supported the authority and independence of the papacy; and the Franconian and Swabian supporters of the imperial house of Hohenstaufen, known jointly as the Ghibellines (from the Italian name for the city of Waiblingen, where many of their most important princes were born), who supported the power of the Holy Roman Emperor at the expense of the papacy. The Guelphs were also supported by the many Italian city-states that no longer wished to be beholden to a German emperor.

After the death of Heinrich V, Germany was torn apart by the squabbling between the noble factions, each of whom supported their own candidate for the throne, the Ghibellines by virtue of election, the Guelphs by virtue of heredity. The disorder in the kingdom grew so pronounced that in 1152 both sides, exhausted, were able to agree on the accession of Friedrich I, a Hohenstaufen closely related to the Guelphs through his mother. Often referred to as Barbarossa (Redbeard), which is what the Italians called him, Friedrich restored peace to Germany and added much of northern Italy, Burgundy, and Bohemia to its dominions. His triumph over his great rival, Heinrich, called Henry the Lion, duke of Saxony and Bavaria—whom he stripped of his feudal lands—was finally achieved through use of the courts rather than an exercise of absolute royal power, a course of action that helped bind Germany's nobles more closely to him. It was during Barbarossa's 38-year reign that the term Holy Roman Empire came into popular usage. One of the most beloved German kings, Friedrich was killed in 1190 while leading a force of 20,000 knights to the Holy Land on the Third Crusade, apparently when he fell from his horse and drowned in a stream. According to German legend, however, he did not die but waits, asleep, in a secret cave deep inside the mountain ridge of the Kyffhäuser, for the moment when he will awaken and restore the empire to its past glory.

Barbarossa's extremely ambitious son, Heinrich VI, concerned himself mainly with increasing the power of the empire in southern Italy. He led no less than six separate military expeditions to Italy and succeeded in having himself crowned king of The Two Sicilies (a kingdom that included the island of Sicily and much of southern Italy), but this was achieved at the expense of a certain neglect of affairs in Germany, where succession quarrels involving the fractious nobility resumed after his death from malaria, at the tender age of 32, in 1197.

Once again Germany descended into civil war between the Guelphs, who held Otto of Brunswick, the son of Henry the Lion, to be the rightful emperor, and the Ghibellines, who supported the candidacy of Philip of Swabia, the brother of Heinrich VI. Otto ultimately won, becoming the only Guelph emperor, but he over-reached himself when he attacked lands the pope claimed as his own. With help from the French, the Ghibellines routed Otto at the Battle of Bouvines in the summer of 1214, and Friedrich II, the grandson of Friedrich Barbarossa, took the throne.

Called by philosopher Friedrich Nietzsche the first European, by his contemporaries *stupor mundi* (the marvel of the world), and by many historians the first modern monarch, Friedrich II was destined to be revered as one of Germany's greatest rulers. Yet, like his uncle Heinrich VI, he was much more concerned with his southern than his northern holdings. In his 35-year reign, which lasted from 1215 to 1250, he visited Germany only 3 times—once for his coronation and then only for a couple of months on 2 other occasions. A poet and scientist, Friedrich II achieved the most in Sicily, his birthplace, where he enacted a number of significant reforms, chief among them the establishment of an efficient, honest, and highly trained government bureaucracy. In 1228, in fulfillment of a vow he had made to the pope, Friedrich II succeeded, through diplomacy backed by the threat of military might, in freeing Jerusalem from the Muslims. Thereafter, however, he continued his predecessors' assaults against Italy, and the papacy came to regard him as a scourge. Nevertheless, during his reign, both the church and the nobility gained in power in Germany. Friedrich II exempted Germany's bishops and other churchmen from the last remnants of lay control, and in the course of reforming the structure of Germany's government, he granted the land's princes increased autonomy over the legislative process, the judiciary, taxes and monetary policy, and the control of roads and byways. At his death in 1250, the medieval German empire had achieved its greatest geographic extent, stretching west to east from the Scheldt and Rhône rivers to beyond the Oder, and from the Baltic and North seas in the north to Italy in the south, where it encompassed all but the Papal States in the center and the northeastern portion of the peninsula.

Albrecht Dürer's engraving Knight, Death, and the Devil *(1513) combines Germanic and Italian Renaissance themes: The Christian knight, who is accompanied by a dog that symbolizes the virtues of untiring zeal, learning, and truth, rides steadfastly toward his destiny, ignoring the figures of Death, on his right, and the Devil, behind him.*

3

The Center Cannot Hold

Germany's great size made it a formidable power, but it also made it extremely difficult to govern. This problem was aggravated by the continuing fragmentation of power in the realm. The death of Friedrich II brought on a new interregnum in which various candidates and their supporting factions struggled for the throne. France, which had begun to fear the potential might of its eastern neighbor, and the papacy collaborated with the German nobles in limiting the power of the emperor. In general, those who succeeded in attaining the German throne at this time concerned themselves more with solidifying their power in their hereditary duchies and principalities than with increasing the strength of the monarchy over Germany as a whole. Although the Golden Bull of 1356 formalized the procedure for electing the Holy Roman Emperor by eliminating the role of the papacy and designating seven electors—the archbishops of Mainz, Cologne, and Trier, the duke of Saxony, the king of Bohemia, the count palatine of the Rhine, and the margrave of Brandenburg; more were added later—this only increased the power of the nobility, for the electors were granted quasi-royal privileges in their respective regions.

As a result, by the mid-14th century, Germany was a collection of literally hundreds of different political entities, ranging in size from larger kingdoms and principalities, such as Bavaria and Brandenburg, to independent cities to tiny baronies that were the minute holdings of thousands of individual free knights, the descendants of a warrior class that owed its loyalty only to the emperor. The steady rise of a merchant class, which of necessity valued stability and coherence in the empire as conducive to the orderly conduct of business, gave rise to new political and economic organizations designed to provide merchants and traders with the protection that might otherwise have been the responsibility of a strong central government. The most significant of these were the various alliances formed by the cities of western and southern Germany against the privations of the knights, whose practice of extorting outrageous toll and highway fees for the use of roads passing through their holdings was particularly damaging to business. The knights formed their own organizations—the leagues of St. George, of St. William, and of the Lion, for example—and the cities and the knights often warred. The other important urban alliance was the Hanseatic League, which was organized by the seafaring merchant towns of northern Germany to protect them against foreign competition and piracy. Bremen, Hamburg, and Lübeck were the most important Hanseatic cities, but in contrast with England and France, where the cities of London and Paris were already becoming truly national metropolises, urban development in Germany mirrored its political fragmentation. A great number of comparatively small cities attained considerable regional significance as economic and cultural centers, but no single city played a dominant role in national affairs. An equally important development that occurred at about this time was the *Drang nach Osten* (drive toward the east), as the eastward migration that nearly doubled the extent of German-inhabited territory was known. By the 14th century, western Germany was heavily populated, and the amount of land available to the peasantry was consequently small. Thus, German peasants were more than willing to settle and develop sparsely populated regions in Austria, Hungary, Bohemia, and Poland.

Despite its political unwieldiness, Germany was both economically and culturally prosperous as the Middle Ages gave way to the Renaissance. Its cities and merchants were well off, and in such cities as Freiburg, Cologne, and Strasbourg the construction of magnificent Gothic cathedrals testified to the vitality of the church. In 1455, in the city of Mainz, a printer named Johannes Gutenberg produced the first book made from movable type, the Bible. Although Gutenberg was forced to sell his famous printing press because of indebtedness, his invention remains one of the most important technological innovations of all ages, because it made possible for the first time the mass production and widespread dissemination of the written word. (In fact, Germany today is a leading exporter of printing and papermaking machines.) Perhaps the strongest evidence of Germany's cultural achievements during this period, however, is the work of its four greatest painters.

Firmly Fixed

Little is known for certain about the artist who survives in history as Matthias Grünewald except for the undeniable power of his masterpieces. It is probable that even the name by which he has come down through the ages is a misnomer; more likely the painter renowned for his stark portrayal of the pain and terror endured by Christ on the Cross at Calvary was born Mathis Gothart Neithart. Grünewald left behind no explanations of his artistic theory, but it is clear that he was uninfluenced by the notions of classical beauty that informed the Italian Renaissance, for he emphasized color and the effects of darkness and light at the expense of anatomical correctness. His greatest work was the

Isenheim Altarpiece, completed in 1515. The central panel of the exterior of the altarpiece, the Crucifixion, is an almost unbearable depiction of Christ's agony. The *Isenheim Altarpiece* was painted for the commandery, or district manor, of the Hospital Order of St. Anthony and was seen by the sufferers of the many diseases treated by the hospital order. Grünewald's Savior is clearly human and has suffered the mortification of torture and a horrible death, but in the work's accompanying panel, the Resurrection, he rises anew, in the full vigor of salvation and clothed in a radiant light. Christ's resurrection is portrayed here as a cataclysm that sweeps the prostrate Roman soldiers and the rocks of the Savior's tomb

Matthias Grünewald's central Crucifixion panel of the Isenheim Altarpiece *(1515) depicts the agony of Christ's tortured death. Grünewald has often been called the last medieval mystic because of his preoccupation with suffering and his vision of a battered world.*

away into the darkness, far from the brilliant halo of the new life. Such is the force of faith in the world, Grünewald clearly says, and like Christ, the sick at the hospital could also be freed of their pain and suffering.

The work of Grünewald's contemporary, Lucas Cranach the Elder, is much less powerful, but it too makes use of brilliant color rather than classical composition to create its effects. In 1505, Cranach became the court painter to Frederick the Wise of Saxony in Wittenberg. Cranach painted a diversity of subjects, including the female nude, mythological and allegorical scenes, and religious works. He painted half-length portraits naturalistically, presenting the figures close to the picture plane, using dramatic landscape as background, and combining a northern accentuation on atmosphere and variety of texture with rich, warm color. Some art historians criticize as superficial Cranach's later work, which was done after he became a sort of court painter for Martin Luther and is more concerned with portraiture, mythology, and history than with overt religious themes. However, Cranach's realistic treatment of nature as encountered in the foothills of the German Alps heralded the development of landscape painting and influenced the type of painting—embraced by the so-called Danube School of artists, including Albrecht Altdorfer—which was characterized by its emphasis on nature rather than figures and objects.

Born in the city of Augsburg in 1497 and settling in Basel around 1514, Hans Holbein the Younger was of a later generation than Grünewald or Cranach. (He was 22 years younger than the former, 25 years younger than the latter.) Perhaps for that reason—the ideas of such masters of the late Italian Renaissance as Leonardo da Vinci, Michelangelo, and Raphael had had more time to filter into Germany—his great early works, such as *The Madonna of Burgomaster Meyer*, completed in 1528, reflect the influence of both the Italian and the northern schools of painting. The Italian emphasis on harmonious composition—that is, the placement of the

Hans Holbein the Younger completed the painting Madonna of Burgomaster Meyer *in 1528; he monumentalized his composition by changing the scale of the figures. Holbein found that there was more opportunity for painting portraiture in England than in Basel and left for London in 1532. He later became court painter for King Henry VIII.*

figures in the painting to achieve a sense of balance and order—is evident in the symmetrical arrangement of the kneeling Meyer family on either side of the standing Virgin Mary, whereas the northern influence can be seen in Holbein's carefully detailed presentation of the contemporary clothing worn by his subjects and in his insistence on a realistic depiction of their facial features, which is much closer to portraiture than the idealized conception of beauty of the Italian masters. Driven from Basel by the religious conflicts that wracked the region through much of the 16th century, Holbein wound up as the court painter of Henry VIII of England; his seemingly simple portraits, characterized by scrupulous fidelity to detail, reveal considerable insight into the character of his sitters. His masterpieces of portraiture include *Erasmus of Rotterdam, Archbishop Warham, Sir Thomas More,* and many paintings of Henry VIII.

If achievement is built on ambition, it is only fitting that Albrecht Dürer (1471–1528), painter, printmaker, and theoretician, should enjoy the high reputation he has claimed for nearly five centuries, for more than any other German artist of the time, Dürer felt keenly what he regarded as the artistic inferiority of the north in comparison with wondrous Italy, and he labored intensely all his life to capture the artistic fire of the Italian geniuses. In 1505, when he left Nuremberg and was received warmly in the Italian city of Venice, the home of his revered masters Titian, Tintoretto, and especially Giovanni Bellini, he exulted. "How I shall shiver for the sun," he wrote in a letter to a friend in Germany. "Here I am a lord, at home a parasite." Yet Dürer's protestations of hostility and indifference on the part of his countrymen ring a distinctly false note, particularly in contrast with the truthfulness of his art. Dürer was Germany's first artistic celebrity, no less lauded in his homeland than he was in Italy and elsewhere on the continent.

For all his admiration of the painters of the south, Dürer is quintessentially a northern artist in that his particular genius most reveals itself in works that reflect his careful observation and detailed re-creation of the natural and material world. Where the Italians strove to represent spiritual truths and to create an ideal conception of beauty (that "certain idea" of beauty that Raphael, for example, held in his mind), Dürer, in watercolors such as *The Hare* and *The Great Piece of Turf*, achieved instead an almost photographically precise depiction of nature. Dürer regarded "a form and figure out of nature with more pleasure than any other, though the thing itself is not necessarily altogether better or worse." For him, nature and beauty were inseparable. "Depart not from nature in your opinions," he advised other artists, "neither imagine that you can invent anything better . . . for art stands firmly fixed in nature, and he who can find it there, he has it." In his woodcuts and engravings, which because they were widely circulated at prices that ordinary people could afford were even

Dürer's watercolor The Hare *(1502) displays the artist's curiosity about nature and his concern with detail; in Dürer's hands, the hare, a small part of nature, becomes a work of art.*

more responsible for his popularity in Germany than his paintings, Dürer showed a similar concern with realistic depiction of detail. The stable in his engraving *Nativity*, completed in 1504, is a tottering, crumbling edifice on its way back to nature; trees grow from a broken outer wall and birds nest atop the loose broken boards that serve it as a roof. Dürer portrayed each crack and chink in the humble structure with careful detail; almost unnoticed, in a rude shed at the lower left, Mary and a shepherd pray over the newborn Christ child. On the surface, there is little of the splendor and magnificence with which a southern artist might have invested a nativity scene, yet a sense of wonder still prevails. Dürer's method reinforces the spiritual content of his message: Amid the modest and timeworn things of this world miracles are born.

The Habsburgs

In 1438, Albert II, a member of the Habsburg family, the ruling house of Austria, was crowned Holy Roman Emperor. Except for two brief interregnums, the Habsburgs would rule the empire until Napoléon Bonaparte dissolved it in 1806. Maximilian I, who ruled from 1493 to 1519, was known as the Last Knight because he was courageous, chivalrous, and a great patron of the arts—Dürer was his court painter. As a result of a series of marital alliances inspired by Maximilian, when Charles V (Karl V, Maximilian I's grandson), the last Holy Roman Emperor to be crowned by a pope, took the throne in 1519, he ruled not only the German-speaking lands but Spain, the Netherlands, and much of Italy.

Somber, diligent, and extremely religious, Charles V may have been the most powerful monarch in Europe, the holder of 75 titles, and the ruler of an empire over which, he said, "the sun never set," but he was unable to achieve centralization of power in Germany. Born and raised in the Netherlands, king of Spain three years before he became Holy Roman Emperor, Charles spent only brief periods in Germany during his lifetime. Larger strategic questions concerned him more than did German reform; he regarded the continued loyalty of the plethora of German principalities to the Habsburgs as being more important than their ability to act in concert in accordance with some notion of German nationhood. Furthermore, when Charles V came to the throne, Germany was being rent by a spiritual schism that would ultimately divide all of Europe.

The Reformation

On October 31, 1517, a 34-year-old priest and professor of biblical studies at the University of Wittenberg named Martin Luther nailed a document, written in Latin, to the door of the castle church in Wittenberg. The document eloquently detailed, in 95 separate points, its author's disagreements with current church practice and doctrine. Widely disseminated by like-minded reformers and scholars, Luther's Ninety-five Theses ignited a religious conflagration that soon engulfed most of the continent.

Luther's chief objection was to the church doctrine of salvation through works, which held that the eternal life of the spirit could be won through moral actions. Over time, this concept had been corrupted to include in meaning and practice the sale of indulgences—literally, papal certificates of redemption for sins. Indulgences were obtained by performing specific devotions, usually to holy relics obtained by princes and church fathers, and by donating prescribed amounts of money. A certain donation bought one, for example, a reduction in the amount of time a soul might otherwise have to spend in purgatory before ascending to heaven. The sale of indulgences preyed upon the piety and fears of the faithful while greatly increasing the power, prestige, and wealth of churchmen.

This practice had been widespread for centuries and had been decried nearly as long, but Luther's protest was timely for several reasons. In the previous decades, the sale of indulgences had reached new heights. Between 1509 and 1520 Luther's own prince—the elector of Saxony, Frederick the Wise—increased his

Martin Luther was a priest and a professor of theology at the University of Wittenberg when he nailed his Ninety-five Theses to the Wittenberg church door in 1517. Luther's list of points attacking the Roman Catholic church's practice of selling indulgences caused a considerable scandal in Germany and led to what is now called the Reformation.

stock of sacred relics from 5,000 to 19,013. These, according to the catalogs he circulated, included a thorn from the crown of thorns worn by Jesus on the cross, a nail that had held him there, a twig from the burning bush of Moses, and four strands of the Virgin Mary's hair. Purchasers of indulgences from Frederick the Wise could obtain remittances of their terms in purgatory of 1,902,202 years and 27 days. The elector used the revenues from the sale of indulgences for, among other things, the operation and improvement of the University of Wittenberg.

Even better bargains were available elsewhere for the shopper eager to ensure favorable future treatment for his or her soul. In 1517, sales agents for the Great Indulgence offered by Pope Leo X fanned out across Germany. The pontiff was in a great hurry to raise funds to finish the construction of St. Peter's Basilica in Rome, and his indulgence promised great dividends. Not only could the purchaser obtain a papal passport to heaven but for an additional fee, retroactive indulgences could be obtained for friends and relatives who had already died and might be suffering the stings of purgatory. A popular rhyme of the day reflected the alleged efficacy of Leo's Great Indulgence:

As soon as the money in the box rings
The soul from purgatory's fire springs

Although Frederick the Wise banned Leo's salesmen from Saxony, it was Leo's indulgence, and in particular the manual of instructions the archbishop of Mainz had prepared for the pope's salesmen, that inspired Luther's wrath. Luther followed his theses with a barrage of pamphlets and dissertations that attacked the corruption of the church, specifically the doctrine of works and the sale of indulgences. He argued that faith alone was sufficient for a person to attain salvation, and he emphasized individual interpretation of the Scriptures. When the pope demanded that Luther recant his accusations, Luther refused and was excommunicated in 1521. Despite calls from church bodies for his seizure and imprisonment, Luther remained safe under the protection of Frederick the Wise.

Following Luther's excommunication, his movement gradually evolved from a quest to reform the Catholic church to the creation of a new, separate, reformed church. The printing press permitted the mass circulation of the unending stream of circulars and broadsides penned by Luther—he published an average of one a month until his death in 1546—and he quickly acquired a wide following. More important, he succeeded in winning the support of a large number of the German princes. Some were motivated by genuine religious conviction, others by the realization that Luther's movement offered the opportunity to create a specifically German church that would bring with its foundation a great reduction in the power of the papacy and Catholic church officials in Germany and a corresponding increase in their own might. For example, Frederick the Wise protected Luther not out of any innate sympathy for his ideas but because he resented the attempts of Rome to dictate the teachings of a professor at his university. Likewise, Frederick had banned the salesmen of the Great Indulgence from his realm not because he opposed indulgences—his coffers were filled with gold florins obtained from their sale—but because he did not want the money usually spent by purchasers in Saxony to go to Rome. Other German princes seized upon the Reformation movement as a pretext to confiscate church lands and break the power of the bishops. Thousands of private citizens were drawn to Lutheranism by the notion of personal freedom seemingly inherent in Luther's espousal of the individual relationship between each human and God, which many interpreted as having profound political ramifications in terms of the relationship between government and the governed. Many believed as well that the overthrow of the spiritual authority of the church heralded a revolution in the relations between master and man. For the most

Pope Leo X, here depicted in a painting by Raphael, was a great patron of the arts, and his reign exemplified the luxury and magnificence of the papacy during the Renaissance. Although he tried, unsuccessfully, to reform the church at the Fifth Lateran Council in Rome, his most famous act was the excommunication of Martin Luther on January 3, 1521.

part, Luther did not share these interpretations and faithfully upheld the authority of the princes. For example, when Germany was convulsed in the mid-1520s by the so-called Peasants' War, in which thousands of peasants, citing Luther as among their inspirations, rose up to shake off the oppression of the nobility, which owned most of Germany's land, Luther responded with a pamphlet, *Against Robbing and Murdering Gangs of Peasants*, that encouraged the princes to be ruthless in crushing the uprisings. You must "smite, strangle, and stab," Luther advised his princely supporters. "It is just as when you must kill a mad dog; if you don't get him, he will kill you."

The staunchly Catholic Charles V initially sought to dismiss the tumult unleashed by Luther as nothing more than a "monks' quarrel," but it more closely resembled a civil war; and by the middle of the 16th century a little more than half of Germany had proclaimed itself Lutheran or one of Lutheranism's Protestant offshoots. In general, the strongest Protestant regions were in the north of Germany, the most ardently Catholic in the south. By virtue of the Peace of Augsburg of 1555, an uneasy truce between the Protestants and the Catholics prevailed—*Cuius regio, eius religio* (In his own realm, his own religion), whereby each prince determined the religious faith of his own people—and the fighting in Germany was halted for several decades.

Luther's Bible

Luther's significance as a literary figure in German history is almost as important as his achievements as a religious reformer, although these two aspects of his life's work cannot really be separated, as they are but opposite sides of the same coin. As the reader has seen, part of the reason that the Reformation spread so quickly and widely was Luther's skill as a writer, his tirelessness as a polemicist, and the availabilty of new technology that made it easy to disseminate his teachings. Central to Luther's thought was the notion that the Bible must be made available to everyone so that each person could come to an individual knowledge and understanding of the Scriptures. Luther saw that because Catholic masses were said in Latin and the Bible was available only in Latin, the word of God was therefore only directly accessible to the most educated members of society—in Germany at the time, a small, elite segment indeed. Most of the people therefore were dependent upon priests for their religious understanding. Luther wanted to change this; the great reformer of Wittenberg believed that the Gospels and the Old Testament should be available to everyone. Accordingly, much of his time and energy was devoted to preparing a German translation of the Bible. Luther's Bible is considered the absolute masterpiece of German prose; its appearance also did more than any other single document to standardize the German language. Its significance in German literature is equivalent to that of the King James Bible in English in that, if only for the sheer beauty and majesty of their language, both are regarded as the supreme evocation in their tongue of the holy truths of the Judeo-Christian tradition.

The Thirty Years' War

The Counter-Reformation, as Catholic Europe's response to the challenge of Protestantism was known, culminated in the carnage and catastrophe of the Thirty Years' War. The war began in about 1618 as a continuation of the ongoing struggle in Germany between the Catholic and Protestant princes, but it soon grew into a larger conflict that brought several of Europe's strongest powers— Protestant England and Sweden, Catholic France—into league with the German Protestants in an effort to limit, if not break, the power of the Habsburg Holy Roman Empire. The war began over the attempts of the Bohemian nobles to overthrow their realm's Catholic king; when the Habsburg forces, through the inspired leadership of such generals as Johann von Tilly and Albrecht von Wallenstein, proved triumphant in the war's early phases, Denmark, and more important, powerful Sweden, entered on the Protestant side. More years of bloodshed followed, until the exhausted combatants agreed upon a peace at Prague in 1635. But for years France had been wary of the increasing power of the Habsburgs, and its chief government minister, the wily and nefarious Cardinal Richelieu, now recognized a prime opportunity to strike against his nemesis. France was fervently Catholic, but Richelieu, a master of *realpolitik* (politics based on practical and material factors), if ever there was one, nevertheless made common cause with the Swedes and the German Protestant princes. The bloodiest phase of the war then ensued, with Spanish forces joining the Habsburg troops and England aiding the anti-imperialist armies until the Treaty of Westphalia ended the war in 1648. The Habsburgs still ruled, but Germany, where virtually all of the fighting had taken place, was prostrate, demolished physically, economically, and spiritually.

It is virtually impossible to overestimate the significance of the Thirty Years' War in relation to Germany's national development. The devastation endured by Germany was truly shattering. The *Soldateska* (soldiers) unleashed upon Germany by their commanders were infamous for their brutality and rapacity. Looting, rape, arson, and other atrocities, directed against civilians as well as combatants, were commonplace. Entire towns were leveled; crops were burned and the countryside was laid waste. Neither side was virtuous in its conduct of the war. In one notable episode, the troops commanded by Tilly, who was known as the Monk in Armor because of his blameless personal life, ran amok on the citizens of Magdeburg, a Protestant town on the Elbe River. When the smoke cleared and the carnage ceased, only 5,000 of the town's 30,000 inhabitants were left alive. Such incidents were the rule rather than the exception. According to historian Gordon Craig, in the last 18 years of the war, Swedish troops alone destroyed 18,000 villages, 1,500 towns, and 200 castles. In one of the great works of German literature from about this time, Hans Jakob Christoffel von Grimmelshausen's picaresque novel *Der Abentheuerliche Simplicissimus* (The Adventurous Simplicissimus), the protagonist tags along with a group of plundering soldiers who "swept through the villages, stole and took what they wanted, mocked and ruined the peasants and violated their maids and wives and daughters and, if the poor peasants didn't like that and dared to be brave and to rap one or the other forager across the knuckles because of their deeds, then one cut them down, if one could catch them, or at least sent their houses up to heaven in smoke." Starvation in the countryside was rampant; in some areas the unfortunate peasants resorted to cannibalism to survive. In Württemberg, the population was reduced from 400,000 to 48,000; Bohemia's populace dwindled from 3 million to 780,000, and at war's end only 5,000 of its 35,000 villages still stood. Overall, the population of Germany dropped from 21 million to 13 million. Germany's economic devastation corresponded to its human loss, and the damage to the nation's collective spiritual and psychological well-being is simply impossible to estimate. It took generations for Germany to recover.

Politically, the consequences for Germany of the Thirty Years' War were almost as great. The anti-imperialist forces had not succeeded in crushing the Habsburgs, but as a result of the Peace of Westphalia, which was proclaimed on October 24, 1648, France emerged as the war's true winner. Recognizing that Germany's continued political fragmentation was of benefit because it prevented Germany from acting as a united power, France established itself as a guarantor of the sovereignty of the individual German states, which after the Peace of Westphalia numbered more than 300. For centuries to come, the rest of Europe regarded German disunity as integral to the balance of power on the continent. In the Peace of Westphalia, Germany was also deprived of control over all its river outlets to the sea. Poland controlled much of the Baltic coastline, Sweden claimed the Oder River and surrounding territory, Denmark governed the right bank of the Elbe, and the Netherlands—whose independence was at last formally recognized—watched over the mouth of the Rhine. At a time when the other European powers, most notably Spain, France, and England, were in the process of developing new trade routes and consolidating vast colonial empires overseas, Germany found itself essentially landlocked.

Friedrich II, called Frederick the Great, (rear center) and the French writer Voltaire (facing Friedrich at left) were good friends; in fact, in 1750, Voltaire came to live at Sans Souci, the king's palace near Potsdam, at Friedrich's request. Friedrich was often called the philosopher-king because he was an intellectual as well as a prolific writer on political matters.

4

The Obedient Land

In the aftermath of the Thirty Years' War, the power of the German princes and nobility increased. The war left the peasantry and middle class devastated, and in the countryside the nobility was able to increase its landholdings at the expense of the lower classes. In most of the German states, the government became highly bureaucratized. Most of these high officials were prominent nobles; below them were educated members of the upper class. There was little opportunity for popular participation in political life; all were beholden to the ruling prince. German society, as countless historians and other observers have remarked upon, became characterized by an extremely high degree of loyalty and obedience to the ruling class. This was not a new phenomenon— one of the popes of the Middle Ages had described Germany as the *terra obedientiae* (Latin for the obedient land)—but in the 17th and 18th centuries it intensified. The greatest catalyst for this change was the national cataclysm Germany had recently endured. In the war's wake, Germans seemed willing to give unquestioning obedience to strong government because it promised the greatest protection against the kind of devastation that they had recently experienced. Over time, obedience and loyalty to government acquired the weight of tradition, cloaked itself in the sanctity of virtue, and became a national characteristic much commented on by outside and German observers alike. Karl Friedrich Moser, a famous German publisher of the Enlightenment, wrote in 1758: "Every nation has its principal motive. In Germany it is obedience; in England, freedom; in Holland, trade; in France, the honor of the King."

Despite its continuing political fragmentation, a new emphasis on the uniqueness and value of things German became evident at about this same time. This trend was particularly pronounced in the so-called German heartland, the region of mid-sized towns and cities set in the countryside that stretched from Westphalia to the Danube and from the Rhine to upper Saxony. This area, as contrasted with Austria and Bavaria to the south and Prussia to the north, was viewed by its inhabitants as the repository of the German essence. Writing in 1865, the great German composer Richard Wagner, who was obsessed with the idea of German identity and whose operas made potent use of German mythology and symbolism, noted: "After the complete destruction of the German essence, after the almost complete extinction of the German nation as a result of the indescribable devastations of the Thirty Years' War, it was this most intimately homely world from which the German spirit was reborn."

The Rise of Prussia

To its European neighbors, this German resurgence took the form of a preoccupation with military concerns, as illustrated by the rise of Prussia, the electorate and then kingdom (from 1701) of northeast Germany that at its greatest territorial extent would constitute two-thirds of the German nation. Prussia's ascension began during the 48-year reign of Friedrich Wilhelm, the Great Elector and the first of the great rulers of the house of Hohenzollern, who

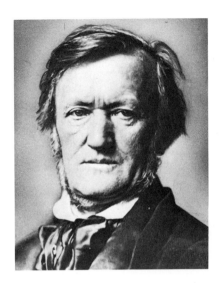

The composer Richard Wagner revolutionized romantic opera in Germany during the second half of the 19th century. He often used German mythology as a basis for his librettos and combined German legends with impassioned romantic music to create highly theatrical operas, including Lohengrin, Tristan und Isolde, *and* Der Ring des Nibelungen.

took the throne as the elector of Brandenburg in 1640. Friedrich Wilhelm succeeded, through force of arms, in reclaiming much of his state from Sweden, which had occupied it during the Thirty Years' War. In 1660, he brought Prussia under his rule. His son, Friedrich I, crowned himself king of Prussia in 1701 and continued the policy of territorial expansion begun by his father, but his achievements paled in comparison with those of his son and successor, Friedrich Wilhelm I, who during his reign, which lasted from 1713 to 1740, increased the Prussian army from 40,000 to 83,000 troops. This gave Prussia the fourth-largest army in Europe, despite its being only 10th in size and 13th in population.

Friedrich II (1740–86)

Friedrich Wilhelm I's army, the pride of Prussia, was inherited and put to use by his son, Friedrich II, known as Frederick the Great. A bookish and somewhat timid child who was easily intimidated by his verbally and physically abusive father, Friedrich II was initially reluctant to inherit the throne and even attempted to escape Prussia, but he was captured and then forced to witness the beheading of his best friend, who had aided him in his plans to flee. After that,

Friedrich II never again attempted to shirk his hereditary obligations. An extremely cultured and refined individual, he befriended and supported the French writer Voltaire, wrote passable poetry, became an accomplished musician, and penned superb essays that attempted to refute the political philosophy of Machiavelli, but as a ruler he was an uncompromising practitioner of power politics whose wars added great expanses of territory to Prussia. At the same time, he instituted a series of sweeping economic and legal reforms that made Prussia one of the most modern and best-governed states of Europe. His victories in the War of the Austrian Succession (1740–48) and the Seven Years' War (1756–63) made Prussia the most feared military power in Europe and left his state and Austria—which was still ruled by his great enemies, the Habsburgs—on a collision course regarding German supremacy.

Napoléon Bonaparte

Despite all his services for Prussia, Friedrich II was an avid Francophile, an admirer of the literature, music, philosophy, art, and especially the language of France, in which his own excellent prose was written. Friedrich II even went so far as to pronounce German culture "vulgar." In the latter half of the 18th century, this admiration for France was shared by many German intellectuals. France was then the center of the intellectual movement known as the Enlightenment, which emphasized the role of reason in ordering and governing human affairs. Voltaire, Friedrich's great friend, was perhaps the most important literary figure in Enlightenment France; Friedrich II, with his domestic emphasis on progress and the rule of law, was the quintessential Enlightenment despot.

Many Enlightenment thinkers, in France and elsewhere, championed democracy; thus, the rise of Napoléon Bonaparte to power in France following the revolution that overthrew the royal family was welcomed by a sizable segment of the German population, who believed that Napoléon would bring democracy to the rest of Europe. Support for Napoléon in Germany was strongest among the intellectuals and those princes who resented the power of the Habsburgs and Prussia. Conversely, Austria and Prussia were among the European states that regarded the French Revolution in general and Napoléon in particular as a diabolical threat to the established order. Both fought against Napoléon's vaunted Grande Armée, which by 1810 had swept over much of Europe, but it was not until Bonaparte overextended himself by invading Russia in 1812 that they were able to make any headway against him. By that point, Napoléon had annexed all of Germany west of the Rhine, abolished the Holy Roman Empire (in 1806), and established in its place the Confederation of the Rhine (Württemberg, Bavaria, Saxony, Westphalia, and 32 smaller principalities that Napoléon had consolidated out of the dozens of German states) under his control.

Following Napoléon's final defeat at Waterloo and permanent exile to St. Helena in 1815, the European nations met at the Austrian city of Vienna to construct a new balance of power for Europe. Both Austria and Prussia (two of the four major powers at the meeting, which also included Russia and Britain) argued against the unification of Germany, which some diplomats favored as a means of holding France in check. Both cited the traditional liberties of the German states as the reason for their opposition, but both were equally moved by their own reluctance to see this theoretical German state dominated by the other. Instead, the diplomats, under the guidance of the Austrian statesman and prince Klemens von Metternich, established the German Confederation, an extremely loose union of the 39 German states (including the four free cities of Hamburg, Bremen, Lübeck, and Frankfurt), each of which was represented in a legislative body known as the Diet. Austria was awarded the permanent chairmanship of the Diet, which was to meet at Frankfurt; Prussia was stripped of much of the territory it had carved away from Poland but was rewarded for its role in defeating Napoléon with much of Saxony and sizable chunks of the Rhineland and Westphalia as well.

In ending Napoléon's 20-year dominance of the Continent (only the Scandinavian nations were not visited by his armies), the diplomats at Vienna tried to restore the old order in Europe, placing the heirs to the hereditary ruling dynasties in France and Spain back on their thrones. In Germany, however, despite the changes wrought by Napoléon, the old order had remained essentially intact.

A Flowering of German Culture

Ironically, as Germany faced the possibility of political extinction during the Napoleonic era, its writers and composers were enhancing its cultural prestige to the extent that the German city of Weimar threatened to outshine Paris, Europe's intellectual capital. It was during this period that the literary powers of the poet, dramatist, and novelist Johann Wolfgang von Goethe and the playwright Friedrich von Schiller, Goethe's close friend, reached

The composer Ludwig van Beethoven (1770–1827) demonstrated that music could be a means of personal expression. He was often described as "half-crazy" because of his oddness, and after he became deaf he was looked upon by many as a tormented musical genius.

their peak. Schiller's greatest play, *Wallenstein*, about the general of the same name from the Thirty Years' War, appeared in 1799, while between 1796 and 1809 Goethe produced his great character study, *The Apprenticeship of Wilhelm Meister*, his psychological novel *Elective Affinities*, and the first part of his epic poem *Faust*. Goethe's earlier novel, *The Sorrows of Young Werther*, the story of a lovesick swain who commits suicide after he is rebuffed by his beloved, heralded much of the sensibility of the German Romantic movement.

The presence of Goethe and Schiller made the city of Weimar the literary capital of Germany, if not of all Europe. Among the other influential German writers who spent time in Weimar were the poet Friedrich Hölderlin and the master of the short story Heinrich von Kleist. The importance of their work aside, their life could have served as inspiration for the German literature of the day, with its emphasis on individual sensibility, heroism, and tragedy. Like characters from a German Romantic poem or novel, both were highly sensitive persons who believed themselves to be greatly misunderstood and who suffered for the sake of their art. Both were also highly individualistic, idiosyncratic writers whose reputation in the 20th century has outshone that which they enjoyed in their own day; both were figures of tragedy whose misfortune curtailed their literary production. Kleist committed suicide at a young age; Hölderlin spent the last 37 years of his life hopelessly insane.

Among the other artistic giants who came to Weimar was the composer Ludwig van Beethoven. Beethoven's great Third Symphony—his favorite symphony, known popularly as the Eroica—was dedicated to Napoléon until the composer, an ardent republican, learned that the Frenchman had proclaimed himself emperor. "Now he too will trample on the rights of man, and indulge only his own ambition," Beethoven thundered as he scratched out the dedication on the title page, his pen raking a hole in the score. A great admirer of Goethe's, Beethoven wrote songs based on several of the writer's poems and composed music for his play *Egmont*. Their characters were incompatible, however; Goethe preferred to maintain a polished, Olympian aloofness, whereas Beethoven was something of an enfant terrible, passionate and unconcerned with the etiquette of high society. Goethe wrote of him, "His talent amazed me; unfortunately he is an utterly untamed personality." A friend described Beethoven as "singing, howling, stamping, looking as if he had been in mortal combat" while composing; a woman whom the composer courted characterized him as "half-crazy." Beethoven's oddness was accentuated by the loss of hearing that began to afflict him sometime around his 30th birthday in 1800 and rendered him totally deaf by the 1820s. It left him more alone than ever with the torments and delights of his muse, but it did not lessen his creative powers. Although his relentless originality could be a trial to his contemporaries—"they are not for you, but for a later age," Beethoven chided a listener who expressed difficulty in understanding one of his quartets—Beethoven's symphonies, sonatas, and quartets, as well as his glorious piece of sacred music *Missa solemnis* (his favorite of all his works), are without equal. After his death in 1827, a throng followed his coffin to the grave. It was an unprecedented public homage for a composer.

1848

In the years following the demise of Napoléon, republican sentiment in Germany, as elsewhere on the Continent, continued to grow. The German princes, like hereditary monarchs elsewhere, alternately cracked down on liberalism and granted concessions when to do so was either absolutely necessary or essentially painless. In 1848, as had happened some 50 years earlier, a revolution in France ignited changes throughout Europe. In February of that

(continued on page 73)

SCENES OF
WEST GERMANY

Overleaf: *The Hauptbahnhof, or main train station, of Hamburg is among Germany's busiest and most efficient railway stations. West Germany had more than 20,000 miles (32,000 kilometers) of railway, 35 percent of which was electrified.*

A streetcar drives through the "federal village" of Bonn. Bonn has been the seat of the federal government since 1949. Bonn is also the birthplace of the composer Ludwig van Beethoven (1770–1827).

A West German enjoys a browse through an international collection of albums at a record store.

At night, West Berlin's Kurfürstendamm, the thoroughfare that has become the center of international life in the city, ripples with neon lighting. The ruin of the neo-Romanesque Kaiser-Wilhelm-Gedächtniskirche (built in memory of Kaiser Wilhelm I in 1895) is kept as a reminder of the destruction of war and stands between the new church and its campanile.

A man and woman work in a field of pansies near Cologne in the Rhine Valley. Among Cologne's prominent industries are chocolate and perfume—the city has given its name to the well-known toilet water Eau de Cologne that was first made by the Italian chemist Giovanni Farina, who settled in Cologne in 1709.

A steelworker wears protective clothing at the Thyssen steel plant in Duisburg, in the industrial region of the Ruhr. Duisburg, located where the Ruhr and Rhine rivers meet, is the largest inland port in Europe; its abundant raw materials, especially iron, have made Duisburg the center of the steel industry.

Students work in their physics class at the Technical University of Berlin (West). After high school students pass their Abitur examination, they are guaranteed admission to a university.

The wildest and steepest bank of the Rhine is the right bank, from Rüdesheim to Koblenz. Each castle, island, and rock along the Rhine has its own tale of chivalry or legend, including (center) the Lorelei rock and (left) Castle Katz (Cat) near St. Goarshausen. Because of the Lorelei's famous echo and its threat to river navigation, it has been immortalized by German poets as a siren who by her song has lured sailors to their death. Castle Katz, whose name derives from its builders, the counts of Katzenelnbogen, is said to have been constructed to counter the Mäuserturm (Mouse Tower) built farther downstream.

Hikers have reached the summit of the Zugspitze (9,721 feet, or 2,963 meters), the highest peak in western Germany. Located in the Bavarian Alps southwest of Garmisch-Partenkirchen, the Zugspitze offers a wondrous panorama of glacial ridges and ski slopes.

The citizens of Altenburg (near Bamberg) raise barricades to try to force the duke to accept a liberal constitution during the German revolution of 1848. The German Confederation met in Frankfurt to unite Germany under a constitutional republican government but failed to do so when Prussia's king Friedrich Wilhelm IV refused to accept restrictions on his absolute power.

(continued from page 64)

year, French republicans overthrew the so-called citizen king, Louis Philippe, and proclaimed a republic. The revolt was followed by similar uprisings in most of the kingdoms of Europe. In Germany, members of all classes took to the streets; the fighting was particularly fierce in Prussia. The stunned princes were forced to grant concessions, and at the insistence of the aroused German populace the Diet of the Confederation was abolished in favor of a popularly elected national assembly. Plans for the establishment of a united, constitutional monarchy were drawn up, but although

28 of the German states approved of the proposal, the two most powerful, Austria and Prussia, proved problematic. The proposal was doomed to failure without the participation of at least one of those two states, but considerable opposition was voiced against including the many non-German subjects of the Habsburgs in the new German state. Furthermore, the compromise solution of simply denying them voting rights and other civil liberties was unacceptable to the republicans because it violated the very principles they had risen up to establish. It was then hoped that Prussia's king, Friedrich Wilhelm IV, could be prevailed upon to accept the crown of a united, constitutional Germany, but the monarch was affronted by the very notion of constitutional checks upon his absolute power. His right to rule was given by God to the Hohenzollerns, Friedrich Wilhelm IV asserted, and he refused to accept "a diadem molded out of the dirt and dregs of revolution, disloyalty, and treason." After Friedrich Wilhelm IV's refusal, the revolution lost its momentum. Little of lasting significance was achieved; ultimately, the Confederation and the Diet were restored under Austria's control, and those rebels who remained discontented were forced into submission at bayonet point.

Blood and Iron

Tragically, when German unification was at last attained, it was achieved not as the product of the movement to establish constitutional republican government but as a consequence of a renewed commitment to authoritarianism in Prussia. In September 1862, King Wilhelm I found himself at an impasse with his country's parliament over the military budget and reorganization of the armed services. Wilhelm I wanted more of his citizenry to serve compulsory periods in the army, and he increased funds to modernize the military; the parliament, known in Prussia as the *Landtag*, opposed both proposals. Neither side was willing to give in, so Wilhelm I summoned the only man he believed could break the deadlock, a 47-year-old civil servant and diplomat, Otto von Bismarck, and named him prime minister.

Bismarck wasted little time in letting the Landtag know how he felt about democracy and legislators who would dare defy the king. "The great questions of the day will not be settled by speeches and majority votes," he told the Prussian parliament in his first address to them, "but by blood and iron." Bismarck believed completely in the authority of the state as represented by the king and even said once, "I feel I am serving God when I serve the King." When the parliament refused to yield on the military budget issue, Bismarck simply dissolved it and governed without legislative authority. The military was enlarged, as Wilhelm I had wished, and under Bismarck's leadership Prussia embarked on an industrialization program that greatly increased its productive capacity.

Bismarck's greatest concern was the expansion of Prussian power. When Austria called for a conference of all the German

Otto von Bismarck, appointed prime minister of Prussia in 1862, took only eight years to unify Germany by blood and iron. Later called the Iron Chancellor, Bismarck dominated the German Reich until he was asked to resign by Kaiser Wilhelm II in 1890.

Helmuth von Moltke, chief of the Prussian army general staff in the war with Austria, planned the Austrian war with amazing precision. He took full advantage of Prussia's rail system and superior weapons technology and kept his forces mobile and ready to attack at a moment's notice. It took Prussia only seven weeks to defeat Austria.

princes and monarchs, Bismarck interpreted it as an attempt to increase Austrian influence at the expense of Prussia and prevailed upon Wilhelm I, who was flattered by Austria's invitation to attend, not to participate. Thereafter, relations between Austria and Prussia deteriorated, a course of affairs encouraged by Bismarck, who recognized that Prussia could only become the indisputable leading power in Germany by reducing Austrian influence. Friction between the two soon led to outright belligerence as Bismarck sought to provoke a war, a stratagem that proved successful in the summer of 1866. Led by the brilliant general Helmuth von Moltke, the Prussian forces—who held a great advantage in firepower because of their modern armaments and in mobility because of the superb Prussian railway system—crushed the Austrians in seven short weeks. Although Bismarck agreed with the famous Prussian military strategist Karl von Clausewitz that war should be conducted ruthlessly—"Nothing should be left an invaded people but their eyes for weeping," he once proclaimed—he also held, as did Clausewitz, that war should be fought to obtain a specific purpose, as a continuation of diplomacy by other means. Accordingly, the peace with Austria was generous, for Bismarck had already obtained what he wanted. Austria surrendered no territory to Prussia, but the German Confederation was dissolved and Austria's influence in German affairs effectively ended.

Bismarck's way was now clear to unify Germany under Prussian control. Victory over Austria had brought with it popularity and acclaim, and a newly formed parliament contained many Bismarck supporters where previously scarcely a one was to be found. Only four German states—Bavaria, Baden, Württemberg, and Hesse-Darmstadt—now remained outside the Prussian orbit, and Bismarck was certain that they would rally round should he succeed in provoking a war with France, which regarded powerful Prussia as a menace. He got his war in the summer of 1870 by releasing to the press a carefully doctored telegram that made it appear as if Wilhelm I had cavalierly delivered a humiliating insult to the French ambassador. Bismarck's famous "Ems telegram" (Ems was the resort town from which the telegram was sent) obtained the desired result, and France attacked Prussia. Like the Austrian forces, the French army was no match for the steely Prussian infantry and the genius of Moltke, but this time it took several months, not several weeks, before Prussia reigned triumphant.

On January 18, 1871, the German Empire was proclaimed in the Hall of Mirrors at Louis XIV's palace of Versailles. Bismarck had indeed obtained his desire, for the four holdout German states had been swept up into the new German empire and Wilhelm I had accepted the crown as the united Germany's *kaiser* (emperor, derived from Caesar). This time, however, many Germans wondered if the cost had been too high. There was little doubt that the unification of Germany was a monumental event. According to the great British statesman Benjamin Disraeli, the war with France and the accompanying unification constituted a "German revolution, a greater political event than the French Revolution of the last century." Disraeli further lamented that "the balance of power has been entirely destroyed." In the center of Europe, Germany, *das Land der Mitte* (the country in the middle), now boasted the most powerful army in the world. Of the European nations, its population was second only to Russia's, and its industrial productivity trailed only that of Great Britain. But Crown Prince Friedrich, the kaiser's son, wondered if Germany's unification had been purchased at a terrible moral expense. "We are no longer looked upon as the innocent victims of wrong, but rather as arrogant victors," the crown prince confided to his diary. Once Germany had been a "nation of thinkers and philosophers, poets and artists, idealists and enthusiasts," he wrote. Now the world regarded it as "only a nation of conquerors and destroyers, to which no pledged word, no treaty, is sacred, and which speaks with rude insolence of those who have done it injury. . . . We are neither loved nor respected, but only feared."

The Iron Chancellor

Bismarck dominated the German Reich (empire) until his removal by Kaiser Wilhelm II in 1890. Although nominally a parliamentary monarchy with a bicameral legislature whose lower house, the *Reichstag*, was elected by universal suffrage for males over 25 years of age, Germany was one of the most autocratic states in Europe. Bismarck, the chancellor, could be removed only by the emperor, and as long as Wilhelm I lived, he continued to place absolute confidence in the architect of German unification. Those who opposed Bismarck realized full well just how much power he commanded. The leader of the socialists, Wilhelm Liebknecht, criticized the Reichstag's lack of influence, calling it the "fig-leaf of absolutism." The historian Theodor Mommsen was even more outspoken in his denunciations of the "pseudo-constitutional absolutism under which we live and which our spineless people has inwardly accepted."

Bismarck was ruthless in stamping out opposition, particularly the Socialists and the Catholics, who were fearless in their resistance to Prussian domination of Germany, but he showed a surprising tactfulness in his foreign diplomacy, which was based on his awareness of the uneasiness that a strong and united Germany roused in the rest of Europe. Thus, even while Germany began to challenge Britain and France by acquiring colonies overseas, in Africa and the South Pacific, Bismarck succeeded in isolating France diplomatically and preventing it from consummating an alliance against Germany. At home, Bismarck's sense of realpolitik enabled him to make concessions that, had they come from anyone else, would have been hailed as triumphs of liberalism—chiefly, the creation of comprehensive social legislation, including state-sponsored health insurance, pensions, and life and disability insurance that were the first of their kind in the world. But even

The territory of Cameroon in west Africa becomes a German colony in 1884. Under Bismarck's guidance, Germany began to compete with Britain and France in acquiring colonies overseas. Unfortunately, the cost of protecting and administering the colonies far exceeded what little trade Germany had with them.

though the German government exhibited such laudable concern for the welfare of its citizens, it continued to deny the vast majority of them any real measure of self-government.

The Great War (1914–18)

Wilhelm II became kaiser in June 1888, 99 days after the death of his grandfather, Wilhelm I. (Wilhelm I's son, Friedrich III, died after only 99 days in power.) He was determined to rule, not merely to reign, and to achieve that end he soon decided that Bismarck would have to go. The nearly 75-year-old Iron Chancellor remained unyielding to the end, boasting that "there is only one master in this country and I am it" and forcing the kaiser to demand his resignation twice before tendering it.

In the two dozen years that followed Bismarck's fall from grace, Germany continued to thrive. Its population increased by a third, to 68 million, its steel production surpassed Great Britain's, and it became one of the world's foremost economic and financial powers. Bismarck had always dealt from strength, but he had been keenly aware of its limits and had always been exceedingly careful to maintain the friendship of Russia, to keep France diplomatically isolated, and to avoid overtly antagonizing Great Britain even while allying Germany with Italy and Austria-Hungary. Kaiser Wilhelm II was less adept at the subtlety of international affairs. He initiated a policy of rapid naval expansion, carried out at the same time that he was joyfully proclaiming Germany's intention to challenge the British Empire for colonies and worldwide influence. His saber rattling drove Britain, France, and Russia into a defensive alliance, the Triple Entente. (Germany's arrangement with its allies was known as the Triple Alliance.) This division of Europe into two hostile camps was something Bismarck had scrupulously tried to prevent.

When the heir to the Austro-Hungarian throne, Archduke Franz Ferdinand, was assassinated by a Serbian extremist in June 1914,

Austria-Hungary, backed by its ally Germany, pressed a series of humiliating demands on Serbia. Russia, which had styled itself as the protector of the Orthodox peoples of the Balkans, pledged its support for Serbia; France assured Russia that should Germany declare war, the French would stand by the Russians. No one was willing to back down, and war was soon declared. Italy and the Ottoman Empire joined Germany and Austria-Hungary; Britain entered the war on the side of France and Russia when the German forces violated Belgium's neutrality on their way to invading France. It is possible that a cautious approach by the governments of any of the belligerent powers might have enabled war to be averted, but none of the parties involved exercised such prudence. Wilhelm, by this point unafraid of provocative gestures, was unwilling to counsel Austria to exercise restraint, and England, France, and Russia welcomed an opportunity to chasten Germany, whose newfound power made it something of an upstart in the eyes of longer established nations.

Bismarck's diplomatic strategy had been based on the premise that a war on two fronts—its eastern and western borders—would be an unmitigated disaster for Germany, but the more reckless diplomacy of Wilhelm II envisioned a scenario under which Germany could triumph in such a struggle, with which it was now faced. This plan called for a lightning attack on and quick victory over the French in the west, after which matériel, manpower, and resources could be shifted to the east for the war with Russia. As chief of staff, Helmuth von Moltke, nephew and heir of the great hero of Bismarck's wars, and then Erich von Falkenhayn attempted to enact this strategy, but the invasion of Belgium and France left Germany's supply lines dangerously overextended and the offensive soon bogged down. Although both sides suffered appalling casualties—for example, the battles of Verdun and the Somme, in early 1916, cost each side 1 million dead or wounded—after Germany's initial thrust, neither was able to gain territory. For three years, between 1914 and 1917, the western front moved less than 10 miles. In the east, Generals Paul von Hindenburg and Erich von Ludendorff led the German forces to a couple of early victories, but the Russians rallied and held.

Because Germany's strategy was predicated on a quick victory, this stalemate was disastrous, as Germany lacked the resources to fight a prolonged two-front war. Recognizing this, Falkenhayn hoped that Germany's diplomats could negotiate a favorable peace. Hindenburg, as chief of the general staff, and Ludendorff, as quartermaster general, succeeded Falkenhayn in early 1917, and were less realistic, believing that the enormous sacrifice of life Germany had already endured could be justified by nothing less than complete victory. Their attempt to impose a naval blockade on their opponents by means of unrestricted submarine warfare directed against the shipping of even neutral nations brought the United States into the war on the side of the Allies (France and Great Britain). By early 1918, despite recent military successes, Germany was exhausted, and even Generals Hindenburg and Ludendorff recognized that defeat was inevitable. Military collapse led to the downfall of the government, as an uprising of workers, joined in some areas by soldiers and sailors, drove Wilhelm II into exile. The terms of the armistice signed by Germany's new republican government on November 11, 1918, called for its complete disarmament; and by the terms of the Treaty of Versailles, signed on June 28, 1919, in the Hall of Mirrors at Versailles, Germany was held responsible for the Great War and called upon to pay $33 billion in reparations to the victorious Allies. It lost all colonies in Africa and the Far East, Alsace-Lorraine, Posen, parts of Schleswig and Silesia, and its coal mines in the Saar basin. The Covenant of the League of Nations was also written into the treaty. The League was created under the leadership of U.S. president Woodrow Wilson, and it was hoped that this international

German troops in trenches take advantage of a lull in the fighting during World War I. The war lasted 4 years, took the lives of millions of Germans, and left millions more wounded.

organization would guarantee the security of all nations by resolving any further threats to peace.

The human cost of the war had been great. Sixty-five percent of Germany's 11 million fighting men had been killed, wounded, captured, or were missing at war's end. For both sides combined, the casualties totaled more than 37 million.

Expressionism

On August 11, 1919, Germany became a constitutional republic. It had been humiliated by defeat, the terms of the Treaty of Versailles, demilitarization, and loss of its colonies. For many, radical solutions seemed to offer the only hope to rebuild Germany. Some advocated the violent overthrow of capitalism, while others turned to extreme nationalism. Expressionism, a movement in art, architecture, literature, and film, reached its peak in Germany in the years after the war and seemed to mirror the extreme emotions prevalent at the time, which were in themselves a response to the traumatic events Germany had recently undergone.

The term *Expressionism* refers to a manner of writing and painting that utilized the distortion and stylization of forms for the purpose of expressing a highly subjective vision of reality. In the German art world, for example, in 1905 a group of artists in Dresden, calling themselves Die Brücke (The Bridge), had taken up a style of painting characterized by strong, violent contrasts in color and the distortion of shapes and proportions of objects. Such artists as Ernst Ludwig Kirchner, Emil Nolde, and Max Pechstein determined to work toward a better future for humanity by using painting as their medium. They were influenced by late medieval German woodcuts and by primitive art, and they emphasized instinct and spontaneity in their works. In 1911, another group of artists, located in Munich, went beyond the precepts of Die Brücke to free art from the constraints of reality and, eventually, opened the way to abstraction. Calling themselves Der Blaue Reiter (The Blue Horseman), Wassily Kandinsky, Franz Marc, and Paul Klee, among others, professed that freedom of experimentation and originality were essential to their aesthetics. In German literature, especially poetry, Expressionism was heavily influenced by the psychological theories of Sigmund Freud and emphasized subconscious emotion, intuition, and memory. Franz Kafka, Georg Trakl, Franz Werfel, and Ernst Stadler were among the writers who examined the themes of death, decay, and the misery of civilization in their works. In architecture, Walter Gropius and others founded a school of architecture and applied arts, called the Bauhaus, at Weimar in 1919. The Bauhaus was instrumental in establishing a relationship between design and industry in which the design process was based on mass production. Students were trained both as designers and craftspeople, and the idea of the cooperation of all the arts to create an "integrated" work of art was revived, as had once been taught by the late 19th-century Englishman William Morris. (In 1925 the Bauhaus was moved to Dessau; it was dissolved in 1933 by the National Socialist regime.)

After the Great War, the medium of film exemplified the climax of expressionistic thought and imagery in Germany. In the film *The Cabinet of Dr. Caligari* (1919), produced by Rudolf Meinert and directed by Robert Wiene, the use of distorted settings—wedge-shaped doors and oblique windows with crooked frames—and heavy shadows created a state of anxiety and terror that intensified the point of view of the major character, who is insane. Unusual camera angles, moving cameras, fast and slow motion, special lighting effects, and exaggerated close-ups are characteristic of German filmmaking during this period. The use of such techniques made *Caligari* a pivotal work in the history of film, and it greatly influenced such important filmmakers as F. W. Murnau (*Nosferatu*, 1922), Fritz Lang (*Dr. Mabuse the Gambler*, 1922), and Paul Leni (*Waxworks*, 1924).

The Weimar Republic (1919–33)

The legislature of the new German republic met at Weimar, thereby consciously associating itself with the glory days of the German cultural revival, but it was plagued with problems from the outset. The revolution that had overthrown Kaiser Wilhelm II left Germany in a state of virtual anarchy, and when the government of the Weimar Republic proved unable to deal effectively with the country's ruinous economic problems, its doom was virtually assured. When, in the years immediately following the war, Weimar resorted to printing unsecured paper money instead of raising taxes to solve its economic problems, catastrophic inflation resulted. The German mark became worthless, ultimately plunging to 4 trillion to a single dollar. Prices rose hourly, and it was not unusual to see a family transporting its entire life savings to the market in a wheelbarrow in order to buy groceries. Personal fortunes were wiped out overnight; scores of banks, businesses, and corporations failed. Perhaps because there was so little tradition of democratic government in Germany, many were unwilling to give

After World War I, the poor in Berlin lined up to receive a free bowl of soup. Germany struggled under the terms of the Treaty of Versailles: It had to pay more than $33 billion in reparations to the Allies; was demilitarized and occupied by foreigners; and suffered from a severe food shortage.

the Weimar Republic much time to cope with the massive and myriad problems it faced. Its failure to restore economic order seemed proof of its ineffectuality to many Germans, and it was argued that what was needed to solve Germany's crisis was strong leadership. The inability of the Weimar leaders to deal with the crisis left them thoroughly discredited, and the election of the nearly 80-year-old field marshal Hindenburg as president in 1925 signaled the onset of a conservative reaction that would ultimately plunge Germany—and the world—into an unspeakable tragedy.

The Third Reich

Hindenburg had survived the Great War and its aftermath with his reputation as a hero unscathed. Seemingly forgotten were the hundreds of thousands of dead in the mud and trenches at Ypres, the Somme, the Marne, and at Verdun; enshrined in legend were his victories at Tannenberg and the Masurian Lakes. Not surprisingly, as president, Hindenburg encouraged this lack of critical reflection on Germany's recent past by propagating the myth that Germany had not been defeated militarily but had been "stabbed in the back"; that is, betrayed by craven politicians into surrendering. This notion did almost as much as the economic crisis, which worsened with the worldwide depression, to discredit the Weimar Republic, for of course it was republicans, not Wilhelm II, who had signed the armistice.

The resentment that Germans felt about being made the scapegoats for the Great War was played upon masterfully by a politician named Adolf Hitler, an Austrian by birth, a failed artist turned spellbinding orator who in 1919 joined the German Workers party, which he unified, built up, and renamed the National Socialist German Workers, or Nazi, party in 1920. A demonic master of group psychology, Hitler convinced his ever-increasing group of supporters that the blame for Germany's current straits belonged elsewhere—with the politicians who had sold it out at the end of World War I; with the leaders of the Allies, who had self-servingly affixed all the blame for the Great War on Germany; with the Communists, who wished to infect Germany with the noxious dogma of Karl Marx, whose doctrine of worker control of the means of production was despised by most Germans; with the Jews, who controlled Germany's finance and were thus deemed responsible for the economic crisis and who were foreigners and outsiders who "tainted" Germany's racial purity. Making cunning use of German myth and legend, Hitler promised a rebirth of German greatness, the creation of a Third Reich that would last 1,000 years. (The Holy Roman Empire, from 962 to 1806 was considered the First German Reich, Bismarck's Second Reich lasted from 1871 to 1918, and Hitler's Third Reich began in 1933.)

The German people were ready to accept any solution that offered an end to their problems and a restoration of Germany's prestige. Democracy, as judged by the performance of the Weimar government, had failed, and communism was anathema to a large

Adolf Hitler passes cheering crowds in Czechoslovakia and merges the country with the Third Reich in 1939. Hitler mesmerized crowds with his fiery speeches and appeared in awe-inspiring theatrical settings, and he launched an intense propaganda campaign to sway the public to his side.

segment of the population. Although Hindenburg was reelected president in 1932—Hitler finished second—it was apparent that the Nazis claimed a great degree of support from all segments of society. In January 1933, Hindenburg, despite severe personal misgivings, asked Hitler to become chancellor, recognizing that the cooperation of the Nazis was necessary if the government was to function at all and hoping that some way could still be found to control Hitler. Two months later, the eligible German electorate voted in the parliamentary elections, giving the Nazis a more than two-to-one advantage over the next most numerous party in the Reichstag, as the Weimar parliament was known. Several weeks later, the Reichstag passed the Enabling Act, which combined with subsequent legislation essentially dissolved the republic and gave Hitler sweeping dictatorial powers. Among the laws that Hitler then promulgated were a series of measures depriving Jews of virtually every civil liberty and privilege. (For purposes of this legislation, even a person who was married to a Jew or who had one Jewish grandparent was defined as a Jew.) Over time, this policy was expanded to a program that called for the systematic imprisonment and murder of every Jew in Germany and, ultimately, on the European continent.

It is certainly beyond the ability of a short work to begin to explain how a nation could have acquiesced in the implementation of such an infernal program. Nevertheless, some attempts must be made. Certainly, many of Hitler's followers assumed that his murderous anti-Semitism was simply rhetoric, calculated to win him the support of those who wished to blame the Jews for Germany's problems. Equally as obvious is that a large segment of German society was anti-Semitic, and the roots of anti-Semitism ran deep. Stripping Jews of all their property, forbidding them to go school or to travel or trade, and seizing all their religious books had been recommended by various factions throughout history. Although prior to Hitler, Germany had been regarded as relatively tolerant in its acceptance of Jews in comparison with many other nations of Europe, the practice of regarding them as something less than human was of long standing. Following the upheaval of the war and the Weimar years, many Germans were apparently willing to countenance the severest measures, including mass murder, against a segment of German society if, as Hitler promised, those measures would restore the Germany they had known. When, by about 1939, it became apparent that Hitler indeed intended to carry out even his most unspeakable plans, Germans were also able to say, many of them proudly, that Hitler had fulfilled all of his other promises as well—he had reduced unemployment, ended the chaos of the Weimar period, strengthened German industry, renounced the Treaty of Versailles, restored the German military, created a new Reich that included the German-speaking peoples of Austria and Czechoslovakia, and presided over a rebirth of German power and prestige. To their nation's eternal shame, for many Germans this justified the *Führer* (leader; the title assumed by Hitler) in all else that he did. For

A banner erected in 1936 by the Nazis in Gryfice in Pomerania (now in northwestern Poland) to boycott the Jews states Germans do not buy from Jews. Many Germans believed that the Jews, who controlled the area of finance, were responsible for the widespread economic depression of the 1930s and that they tainted Germany's racial purity. By the end of World War II in 1945, the Nazis' program of genocide had taken the lives of more than 6 million Jews.

others, by the time that they awoke to the full horror of what had occurred, it was too late—Hitler was too firmly entrenched in power. Some were simply too frightened to speak out or resist. Still others professed ignorance, claiming that no one really knew about the concentration camps. It should also be noted that there were many very brave Germans who did resist Hitler. This resistance took the form of both public opposition and private acts of almost unfathomable courage. Nevertheless, the opposition was always very small, and the sheer magnitude of what Hitler's Germany carried out—war against most of Europe and the United States and the systematic extermination of 6 million Jews, along with Poles, gypsies, and other groups considered inferior—could not have been acccomplished without widespread acceptance at all levels of society.

Hitler's conception of his Reich included Austria and the German-speaking territory of Czechoslovakia, so in 1939 he convinced Austria to reunite with Germany and cajoled the leaders of Britain, France, and Italy to agree to his seizure of the Sudetenland, as the predominantly German section of Czechoslovakia was known. Still not content, in September 1939 Hitler invaded Poland, which prompted Britain and France to declare war on Germany. (*Blitzkrieg*, or lightning war, was the term German war strategists used to describe the military tactics they first developed in the Spanish Civil War in 1938 and then used in Poland; by employing tanks and dive bombers to destroy railroads, highways, factories, and cities the Germans hoped to cause psychological shock and confusion in the enemy forces, thereby disabling them by surprise, speed, and superior firepower.) France fell quickly, but Britain struggled on alone until Hitler's invasion of the Soviet Union brought that nation into the war. The United States entered the war in December 1941 following a sneak attack on Pearl Harbor, Hawaii, by Japan, Germany's ally. As powerful as it was, Germany did not possess the industrial capacity to support a war of such magnitude, particularly because Hitler had initiated the conflict without shifting his industrial sector to a wartime footing, believing that his opponents would quickly be defeated. Increasingly unresponsive to the objective military situation, Hitler insisted that Germany fight to the death. By the spring of 1945, the Stunde Null was rapidly approaching. Russian forces were advancing across Germany from the east; American, British, and French forces drove the retreating Nazi troops before them from the west. From his fortified bunker in Berlin, Hitler presided over the collapse of the Third Reich. On April 29, he married his longtime mistress, Eva Braun, in the bunker; the following day, the two of them took a fatal dose of poison. Germany capitulated a few days later.

Jubilant Berliners wave to a U.S. Air Force transport plane as it airlifts supplies to the city. In 1948, in retaliation for currency reforms introduced in West Germany and the western sectors of Berlin by the Allies, the Soviets blockaded the roads leading to Berlin. The Allied airlift, which lasted more than 11 months, carried nearly 1.6 million tons of food, clothing, medicine, and coal to the beleaguered city.

5

From the Rubble

West Germany was born from the smoldering rubble of postwar Germany. At war's end, with its cities demolished, its economy ruined, and millions of its citizens homeless and starving, Germany was occupied by the four victorious Allied powers—the United States, France, Great Britain, and the Soviet Union. The country was then partitioned into four quarters; the capital city of Berlin, although located deep within the Soviet zone, was likewise divided into four. But the end of World War II brought not peace but the beginning of a new struggle—the cold war between the democratic, capitalist West and the communist, totalitarian East. One of the first battles of this conflict was to be fought over Germany.

What to Do with the Germans

Initially, the Allies had agreed, as had Germany's opponents in the past, on the necessity for measures to ensure that the Germans would never again possess the ability to carry out aggressive war against the rest of Europe. For a time, the United States, which emerged from World War II as the strongest of the victors, contemplated imposing the Morgenthau Plan, so called after its creator, Henry Morgenthau, Jr., secretary of the Treasury for 12 years under President Franklin D. Roosevelt. Morgenthau proposed that Germany's industrial capacity be permanently crippled by the dismantling of all its factories and industrial plants. He envisoned a pastoral Germany in which agriculture would be dominant, reasoning that a nation without the ability to mass produce armaments, matériel, and other industrial goods could never contemplate waging war. However, as it became apparent that Joseph Stalin, the leader of the Soviet Union, intended to transform most of Eastern Europe into Communist satellites of his nation, the Allied emphasis shifted to helping Germany recover its economic health, with the eventual goal of bringing it into the Western orbit. The best guarantee of protection against future German aggression, held this new line of thinking, was to make sure that a prosperous postwar Germany developed along genuinely democratic lines. One implication of this policy was the belief that given the opportunity to exercise democratic privileges, the German people would opt for peace. A program of denazification, designed to remove from positions of responsibility all persons with past Nazi ties, was introduced, although its effectiveness varied from area to area. All the Allies also cooperated in carrying out the war crimes trials at Nuremberg, at which 12 of Hitler's leading advisers were sentenced to death.

Because Stalin had no intention of allowing a revitalized Germany to align itself with the West, a break between the Allies was inevitable. The immediate cause of the Western rupture with the Soviet Union over Germany was the issue of currency and price controls. As had been the case in the early days of the Weimar Republic, Germany's economy was in chaos. Germans had no faith in the currency, mainly because there was little to buy. Hoarding was rampant and food was scarce; what little there was could only be obtained on the black market. American cigarettes became the common means of exchange. Although much of Germany's productive capacity remained intact, economic incentive was dampened by the stringent wage and price controls that remained from the Nazi era.

The Allies recognized that currency reform was necessary to stabilize the economy, but it was a German named Ludwig Erhard, one of a number of remarkable postwar leaders with which West Germany was blessed, who was most responsible for the policies that enabled the West German economy to make its miraculous recovery. Economic director of the British and American occupied zones, with which the French soon merged, Erhard overcame the skepticism of the Americans and insisted that all price controls and rationing be eliminated. Both measures were at first extremely unpopular, for Germans were allowed to exchange—at an unfavorable rate—only a limited amount of their old currency, the reichsmark, for the new currency, the deutsche mark, which meant that whatever savings they possessed quickly became worthless. At the same time, the transition from a state-directed to a free-market economy initially resulted in even greater shortages and higher prices, but these quickly gave way to stability, renewed productivity, and full employment. In 1948, the first year of the reforms, production rose by 50 percent; it increased by 25 percent again the following year. According to economist Henry Wallich, the new policies "transformed the German scene from one day to the next. . . . Goods reappeared in the stores, money resumed its normal function, the black and gray markets reverted to a minor role, foraging trips to the country ceased, labor productivity increased, and output took off on its great upward surge. The spirit of the country changed overnight. The gray, hungry, dead-looking figures wandering about the streets in their everlasting search for food came to life." The road was paved for the economic miracle, the *Wirtschaftswunder*, that would stun the world. Even more important, from Erhard's view, was the role that the free-market economy played in preparing the Germans for democracy. "Only when every German can freely choose what work he will do and can freely decide what goods he will consume will our people be free to play an active role in the political life of our country," he had said in announcing the new measures.

Divided Once More

With cause, the Soviet Union regarded the new economic policy as the first step toward unification of the Western Allied zones. They responded by cutting off all land routes into the West, or Allied, section of Berlin in 1948. At first, the Western powers were uncertain about how to respond to the Soviet provocation, but the defiance of the acting mayor of Berlin, Ernst Reuter, helped convince them to airlift food and other necessities to the beleaguered Berliners. By the time the Soviets lifted the blockade of Berlin, in the spring of 1949, the Allies and most Germans had become convinced of the impossibility of immediately reunifying Ger-

In 1949, a bicyclist stops to look at the boundary notice in the British sector of Berlin near the Brandenburg Gate. At the Potsdam Conference at the end of World War II, Germany was divided into four sectors—eastern Germany was assigned to the Soviet Union, northwestern Germany to Britain, southwestern Germany to the United States, and France received the postwar state of Baden and the Saar region. Berlin was also divided among the Allies.

many. Germany was soon divided once more, this time into two sovereign nations—the Federal Republic of Germany, usually referred to as West Germany (with its capital at Bonn), and the German Democratic Republic, popularly known as East Germany (with its capital at Berlin). At the conclusion of World War II, much of the easternmost territory that had long been claimed by Germany had been returned to Poland or Czechoslovakia or had been annexed by the Soviet Union. Of what remained, West Germany occupied slightly more than two-thirds—about 96,000 square miles (248,640 square kilometers). East Germany covered about 41,000 square miles (106,190 square kilometers). Forty-seven million people made their home in West Germany; 18 million lived in East Germany. Every fifth member of the West German population was a refugee, either from East Germany or from the former German regions farther to the east. This exodus from East Germany to its western counterpart remained constant throughout the 41-year history of West Germany, which makes its economic recovery that much more remarkable.

Rebuilding Wealth and Trust

West Germany's constitution, known as the Basic Law, was conceived by its creators, and was so understood in the following years, to be a transitional arrangement until German reunification could be achieved. However, in the spring of 1990, the newly elected conservative government in East Germany indicated its desire that reunification take place under the terms of the Basic Law, which may well become the constitution of a reunited Germany.

The Basic Law calls for a federal German state, the *Bundestaat*, governed by a parliamentary system. The legislature consists of two houses, the *Bundestag*, which is the lower house and represents the popular will, and the *Bundesrat*, which is the upper house and represents the 10 West German states, or *Länder*. Election to the

Bundestag is by popular sovereignty; all individuals over the age of 18 are eligible to vote. The parliament of each *Land* (state), known as the *Landtag*, appoints its delegation to the Bundesrat. The size of each delegation depends on the population of its Land. Although prior to unification West Berlin sent delegates to both houses, they were not allowed to vote. The Bundestag is the more powerful of the two chambers, but the Bundesrat must approve any bill that affects the administrative responsibilities of the Länder, and it may recommend revisions in any government bill.

The head of the West German government was the chancellor, who was the head of the party or coalition of parties that commanded a working majority in the Bundestag. His government, consisting of himself and his ministers, who were usually members of the Bundestag, remained in power only so long as that majority was maintained. Under the Basic Law, the head of the West German state was the president, who was elected by direct popular vote. The president served a five-year term and could succeed himself or herself only once. The president's powers were severely limited—chancellor was the much more important position—but in the past the president was, by force of example and moral weight, able to exercise important leadership. West Germany's first president, Theodor Heuss, was most notable in this regard. One of the architects of the Basic Law, Heuss was successful in setting himself above partisan politics in order to warn more effectively of the many pitfalls that lay along the road to political, economic, and moral rehabilitation. "External power has been gambled away," he reminded Germans upon taking office. "Moral power must be won." His example, like that of Reuter, did much to convince skeptics in other nations about the sincerity of the German commitment to democracy.

Two parties dominated West German politics—the Social Democratic party (Sozialdemokratische Partei Deutschlands, or SPD), and the Christian Democratic Union (Christlich-Demok-

In 1945, eastern German refugees fill the streets of Berlin, temporarily settling among the ruins of the city. Three years later, when the Allies lifted economic controls over western Germany, new stability, productivity, and employment brought the country back to life.

ratische Union, or CDU). All of the West German chancellors came from one of these two parties. A third party, the Free Democratic party (Freie Demokratische Partei, or FDP), although traditionally claiming a much smaller membership than the other two, often made the difference in breaking parliamentary deadlocks. The SPD is the older of the two major parties and can trace its origins to 1875. Year after year, it draws its greatest support from the working class. During the Nazi period, it was targeted for elimination by Hitler, and the architect of its rebirth after the war, Kurt Schumacher, spent 12 years in a concentration camp. In the first years of the Federal German Republic, this history of opposition served the SPD in good stead, but many voters were scared away from it because of its espousal of socialist doctrines, which they believed indicated an unwelcome friendship with the Soviet Union. In 1959 the SPD abandoned its commitment to full socialism and avowed the virtues of private enterprise, although it maintained its commitment to the government's role in providing for an equitable distribution of wealth.

The first chancellor of West Germany, Konrad Adenauer, was the leader of the CDU, which to this day draws most of its support from Catholics. Protestants and Catholics each constituted about 50 percent of the West German population (virtually all of Germany's Jews were either exterminated or had emigrated, mostly to Israel), but Protestants constituted only one-third of the CDU's members. Adenauer, who served as chancellor from 1949 to 1963, was at the time of his first election 73 years old. The former mayor of Cologne and a member of the Reichstag during the Weimar years, Adenauer had himself been imprisoned by Hitler. Together with his colleague Erhard, Adenauer implemented the *Soziale Marktwirtschaft*, or socially responsive free-market economy, which combined the principles of the free-market economy with the idea of judicious government intervention when necessary. Integral to this program was the concept of *Mitbestimmungsrecht*, or codetermination, which held that management and labor should consider themselves partners in industry. Under Adenauer, the West German economy thrived. Despite the challenge of feeding, clothing, and housing millions of refugees from the east, the economic miracle saw national income rise 112 percent and wages increase 119 percent by 1956. The gross national product (GNP), the measure per individual of the total value of the goods and services produced by West Germany in a year, trebled between 1950 and 1964; total industrial output increased sixfold. By 1960, unemployment was less than one percent, and for every person who wanted a job, there were seven unfilled. At the same time, Adenauer's government was able to provide its citizens with comprehensive social benefits that included health insurance, pensions, unemployment benefits, and free health care. The economic miracle fed on itself; as the average German became more prosperous, he or she was able to consider purchasing items previously thought of as luxuries—cars, televisions, and other electronic equipment—and industries that catered to this new demand, particularly West Germany's justly acclaimed manufacturers of luxury cars, prospered accordingly.

Adenauer achieved equal success in international affairs, which were, in fact, his first concern. (For the most part, he gave Erhard a free hand on domestic and economic issues.) A staunch anti-Communist who believed that the left was partly to blame for Hitler's rise, Adenauer emphasized from the outset that Germany's future was with the West. Although sometimes criticized at home for this orientation, which was held to be insufficiently pro-German, Adenauer believed that future peace in Europe depended upon the ability of its nations, most especially his own, to transcend the often belligerent nationalism of the past. To that end, he tried to involve Germany in such multinational arrangements as the Coal and Steel Community and the European Defense Community. Although he enjoyed only partial success,

Konrad Adenauer, the first chancellor of West Germany and leader of the Christian Democratic Union, set in motion the programs of a "socially responsive free-market economy" and codetermination, in which management and labor become partners in industry.

such programs formed the basis for the idea of European unity that proponents hope will be finally realized with the formation of the European Community in the early 1990s. Perhaps Adenauer's most important contribution was his insistence on the need for Germany to break with those elements of the past that had led it to disaster. "When you fall from the heights as we Germans have done," he said, "you realize that it is necessary to break with what has been. We cannot live fruitfully with false illusions." One way in which he hoped to usher in a new age for the Germans was by ending the centuries-old enmity between his nation and France. Early in his years as chancellor, Adenauer stated that "the Franco-German antagonism, which has dominated European politics for hundreds of years and given occasion for so many wars and so much destruction and bloodshed, must finally be removed from the world," and in 1962 he signed a treaty of friendship with France. Equally significant were Adenauer's overtures to Israel, the Jewish homeland created in the aftermath of World War II. On behalf of Germany, Adenauer apologized to the world's Jews for the Holocaust, or "wholesale burning," and committed his nation to paying Israel significant reparations for the war crimes of the Nazis. (By contrast, East Germany offered its first apology only in the spring of 1990, on the verge of its dissolution, and has never paid reparations.)

Largely because of Adenauer's leadership, West Germany quickly gained the confidence of the Western powers, and in 1955 the occupation officially ended. West Germany now became a fully independent state, recognized as such by most of the other nations of the world (including the Soviet Union, but not for some years by East Germany). It was even allowed to raise and maintain an army of up to 500,000 men. Upon reunification, the West German army, the *Bundeswehr*, was the largest and one of the best-equipped in Western Europe, possessing nuclear capability but not nuclear weapons. A united Germany remains, as West Ger-

The Bundeswehr, or the Federal Armed Forces, practices maneuvers. After occupation of West Germany officially ended in 1955, the country was allowed to raise and maintain troops of up to 500,000 men. The Bundeswehr was the largest army in Western Europe and possessed nuclear capability, although it did not have nuclear weapons.

many had been since the end of the occupation, an important member of the North Atlantic Treaty Organization (NATO), the mutual defense alliance of the Western nations. But Adenauer regretted that West Germany was forced to raise its own armed forces—he had hoped instead for the creation of a multinational European army—and his most important legacy is that at a most critical time in German history he demonstrated to his compatriots that democracy did not rule out strong leadership and constantly emphasized the need to look beyond nationalist and militarist solutions. As the historian Gordon Craig has eloquently observed, Adenauer "was the first German statesman who was able to over-come the unconscious tendency of his countrymen to believe that leaders could only be taken seriously when they wore uniforms."

Rebuilding Bridges

After Adenauer left office in 1963, he was succeeded by his colleague Erhard. Ironically, given Erhard's achievements in bringing about the economic miracle, during his term West Germany experienced its first serious economic downturn of the postwar years. A coalition of the CDU and the SPD, headed by Kurt George Kiesinger, succeeded Erhard's government and governed West Germany between 1967 and 1969, when it gave way to the SPD in coalition with the FDP. The new chancellor was Willy Brandt, who had been the mayor of West Berlin in 1961, when the East German authorities had constructed the Berlin Wall in an attempt to halt the ongoing exodus of refugees to the West. (By 1961, nearly 4,000 people a week were fleeing East Berlin.) A charismatic figure who had been exiled in the 1930s because of his opposition to Hitler, Brandt came to office determined to repair relations with East Germany. The success of Brandt's *Ostpolitik* (eastern policy) won him the Nobel Peace Prize in 1971 and brought about recognition of each other's sovereignty on the part of both Germanys. (Previously, both governments had refused to accept the legitimacy of the other.) Although Brandt was forced to resign from office in

Willy Brandt, who served as mayor of West Berlin and opposed the East German Communists and the construction of the Berlin Wall, became chancellor of West Germany in 1969. The first Social Democrat to become chancellor, Brandt won the Nobel Peace Prize in 1971 for his efforts to improve Western relations with the Soviets and the East Germans.

1974 after it was discovered that one of his closest aides was a longtime spy for East Germany, the SPD retained power for six more years under the strong leadership of Helmut Schmidt. Dissatisfaction with the SPD's management of the economy, which suffered from relatively high inflation and unemployment at the beginning of the 1980s, brought the CDU back to power in 1982, with the Rhinelander Helmut Kohl as chancellor. Environmental questions and debate over the positioning of additional nuclear weapons on West German soil were the crucial issues of the early Kohl years, but the heady changes that took place in Europe at the end of the decade made it likely that Kohl will fulfill his professed desire to be remembered in history as the "reunification chancellor." Kohl was the primary instigator for the merging of the two Germanys' currencies and economies; on July 1, 1990, the West German Bundesbank began to have monetary responsibility for East and West Germany. On October 2, 1990, the eve of reunification, the commanders of the Allied forces terminated their occupation of West Germany and West Berlin. The federal government in Bonn, however, had requested that French, British, and American troops remain in the western part of Berlin until the Soviet Union completed the withdrawal of its army from East Germany over the next four years. And on October 3, hundreds of thousands of Germans celebrated their first national holiday of a unified Germany. Moreover, in December 1990, the first all-German parliamentary elections will amount to political reunification and, perhaps, with this unity will come "normal" relations with the rest of Europe.

The Old Music Hall is dwarfed by a new high rise in Hamburg. Hamburg, Germany's second largest city after Berlin and located on the Elbe River, became an important town in the Hanseatic League during the Middle Ages. During World War II, much of the city was destroyed and rebuilt; today, it is a busy port city and shipbuilding center.

6

The Country and Its People

Prior to October 3, 1990, when it reunited with the eastern portion of the German nation, the Federal Republic of Germany was a country of more than 62 million people. The exact number is unknown, for the thousands of refugees who poured into West Germany after the prohibitions against travel between the two countries had been lifted overwhelmed the ability of the authorities to keep count. That population lived on a land area of about 95,929 square miles (248,454 square kilometers); about 45 million West Germans—75 percent of the population—lived in urban areas. Reunification has added about 17 million people—less the number of refugees—to West Germany and a land area totalling almost 42,000 square miles (108,780 square kilometers).

West Germany was composed of three distinct topographical regions—the southern highlands, which includes the Alps, Europe's greatest mountain chain and the site of Germany's highest peak, the Zugspitze; the central uplands, a region of plateaus, hills, forests, and river valleys that is still the most typical of the German landscape; and the northern lowland, which reaches 115 miles (185 kilometers) from the central uplands to the coast of the Baltic and

North seas. By far the most important interior waterway is the Rhine River, which, with its handsome valley dotted with ancient castles, was a traditional setting of German folklore. Navigable almost its entire 700-mile (1,129-kilometer) length, the Rhine continues to be central to the German economy. A tributary on its right bank, the Ruhr River, cuts a valley that is the most important industrial and coal-mining region in all of Germany, if not in all of Europe. The Moselle River, another tributary of the Rhine, flows north from the northeastern part of France to the German city of Trier and joins the Rhine at the city of Koblenz. Since the completion of the Moselle Canal in 1964, the Moselle has been one of the major water routes from Lorraine to the Ruhr. Moselle vineyards are located along the river below Koblenz and produce the celebrated Riesling grape that is used to make the light, dry white wines of the region. Other important rivers of western Germany are the Weser and Elbe, although these two waterways are not as important for commerce, in part because, unlike the Rhine, they are not fed by spring and summer runoff from the Alps and are therefore often too low to successfully navigate.

The climate in western Germany is usually temperate; the far west experiences mild winters and summers because of the moist, warm winds that blow in from the Atlantic Ocean. The average temperature in the northwest is about 50° F (10° C), whereas the southwest averages 53° F (12° C) annually. The east has colder winters and short, hot summers; annual temperatures average around four degrees lower than in the west.

Because western Germany is a heavily industrial, densely populated nation, its environment has suffered. Despite the prevalence of the forest as a setting and theme in much of German literature, particularly its fairy tales and folktales, little of the original woodlands that covered Germany remains. Stands of birch and Scotch pine have replaced the oak forests that were once prevalent in the north, although in the uplands—including the Westerwald,

The Ruhr valley is the most important industrial and coal-mining region in Germany and probably in all of Europe. Steel production is concentrated in vast facilities such as the one pictured here, the Thyssen plant in Duisburg.

Thüringer Wald (Thuringian Forest), Weser Mountains, and Harz Mountains—and the Alps, the Black Forest, and the Swabian Jura, some large forests of beech, silver fir, and spruce still thrive. Deer, red squirrel, wild boar, and fox can still be found in the woods; hare and other small rodents, such as the dormouse and hamster, are also abundant; and, in the valley of the Elbe, beaver continue to be plentiful. Such birds as the gray shrike, thrush nightingale, and nutcracker abound in the north and southeast. Fruit trees, including plum, cherry, and apple, line many of the roadways of southern Germany.

In the area of agricultural production, wheat, oats, barley, rye, potatoes, and beets are grown in the greatest quantities; in the field of animal husbandry, cattle farming and the raising of pigs supply almost 80 percent of the country's needs.

Like most of the world's industrial regions, western Germany faces a serious pollution problem. Industrial waste and fuel emissions have greatly harmed the forests, rivers, and atmosphere, and environmental issues have come to play a large role in German

Ramsau, near Berchtesgaden and not far from the German Alpine Road, lies nestled in the Bavarian Alps. The region surrounding Berchtesgaden is famous for its mountain scenery and salt mines.

politics. The rise of the leftist Green party, founded in 1980, which usually wins enough votes to send a small delegation to the Bundestag, is in a large part attributable to its success in increasing Germans' awareness of environmental concerns.

A Land of Diversity

For political purposes, West Germany was divided into 10 states, or Länder: Baden-Württemberg, Bavaria, Bremen, Hamburg, Hesse, Lower Saxony, North Rhine–Westphalia, Rhineland-Palatinate, Saarland, and Schleswig-Holstein. Although often listed as an 11th state, West Berlin sent a delegation to the lower house in the Bundestag but did not officially possess the status of a Land. Bavaria had the largest area, nearly one-third larger than the next in size, North Rhine–Westphalia, which was the most populous. The smallest Land, both in size and population, was Bremen, the old Hanseatic city; the city of Hamburg also constituted a Land.

Contrary to stereotype, western Germany is a region of considerable diversity. This is perhaps not so surprising when one considers Germany's long history of fragmentation and decentralization. These differences are first apparent to the eye. Southern Germany is the land seen on postcards and travel brochures—a picturesque region of castles, forested hillsides, old churches, and vineyards, whereas the charms of the north, a region of cold winters and windswept flatlands, are less immediately obvious. The south is very much a part of the interior of the Continent, and the traditional German connection with Austria is very apparent there; in the north, the focus is on the sea.

In the north, the daily menu includes a variety of green vegetables and fresh meat, especially mutton. Saltwater fish, such as cod, redfish, shrimp, and flounder, are also in abundance. In the south, there is a wide range of *wurst*, or sausage; ham, pork, potatoes; dumplings, called *Knödel*; and *Spätzle*, or noodles. Both regions are noted for freshly baked breads and rolls, called *Brötchen*. *Mittagessen*, or lunch, is the largest meal of the day; *Abendessen*, the evening meal, usually includes a plate of cold cuts.

There are other differences between north and south that are not as readily apparent to surface observation. The north is predom-

Nets are set for catching eels along the North Sea coast in Schleswig-Holstein. The northernmost state in western Germany, Schleswig-Holstein is bounded on the west by the North Sea, on the north by Denmark, on the east by the Baltic Sea, and on the south by the Elbe River.

inantly Protestant, the south Catholic; and the north tends to be more liberal politically. Although Germany possesses none of the considerable ethnic diversity of, say, the United States, there is said to be considerable difference in character and temperament among Germans from different regions. Stereotypically, Germans from the south are thought to be more emotional, outgoing, convivial, possessed of the indefinable quality Germans call *Gemütlichkeit*, or good-naturedness—the genial Germans of the beer hall and Oktoberfest. The people of the north are believed to be more stolid and reserved, businesslike and frugal. Northerners are more likely to be tall and blond, southerners to be shorter and darker. There are regional differences in language as well. Although everyone uses German to converse and write in, with the exception of the *Gastarbeiter*, or guest workers from foreign nations, the various dialects of German vary considerably. Public discourse on the national level is usually conducted in *Hochdeutsch*, or High German; this is the language as taught in school, the literary language whose primary source is Luther's Bible. But within western Germany, and even within various localities, any number of dialects are used for daily speech, to the extent that a German from Swabia, for example, might have some degree of difficulty understanding a conversation in the dialect of Berlin. Some of these dialects, such as the *Plattdeutsch*, or Low German, spoken in the north, are almost separate languages; Plattdeutsch, for one, is closely related to Dutch.

Small Cities

Although Germany is heavily urbanized, its western region contains many small cities, each of which plays an important regional and national role but none of which is a truly dominant national center in the way that London or Paris is. This, again, is most likely a reflection of Germany's relatively late national development. Although there were 14 West German cities with a population

Gastarbeiter, or guest workers, from Italy package chocolates in a factory in Cologne. Among the Gastarbeiter in Germany today are Turks, Yugoslavs, Italians, Greeks, and Iberians.

of more than 400,000, only that of West Berlin exceeded 2 million, and the combined population of the 4 largest West German cities—West Berlin, Hamburg, Munich, and Cologne—did not equal that of London, Paris, or New York. Bonn, the nation's capital, was only the 19th in terms of population. The tendency toward regionalism means that there is   considerable diversification within the urban economy. Frankfurt is Germany's banking center, whereas the film industry is centered in Munich and Berlin, some of the most important magazines are published in Hamburg, the most prestigious art dealers are in Cologne, the fashion world focuses on Munich, one of the two important television networks broadcasts from Mainz, and the trade union federation has its headquarters at Düsseldorf.

The Village of a Million

Germans sometimes refer to Munich, the prosperous, traditional capital city of Bavaria, home to Henry the Lion and the first headquarters of Hitler's National Socialist party, as the Village of a Million. Home to the giant electronics firm of Siemens, the aerospace contractor MBB, and the world-famous auto manufacturer BMW (Bayerische Motoren Werke, or Bavarian Motor Works), Munich is an economic hub that, somewhat unusually for a German city, draws workers from all around the nation. Most of its residents are not native-born, and according to opinion polls it is the city where most Germans would prefer to live if they left their own. Its preeminence in West German economic and cultural affairs had led to its being dubbed West Germany's secret capital. Munich was home to Germany's best classical opera company, as well to some of its finest collections of art, such as the Alte Pinakothek, the Bayerisches Nationalmuseum, and the Städtische Galerie. Although tourists at Munich's annual Oktoberfest, an internationally known exercise in Teutonic revelry, are likely to encounter beer-quaffing natives attired in the traditional lederhosen (short pants of leather) and green felt hat with a feather, or the dirndl (a dress of colorful material with a tight bodice and full-cut skirt), Munich can also boast of a much more sophisticated nightlife, centered around its fashionable cafés. Some of Germany's most elegant boutiques are also to be found there, as are the nation's finest sports facilities, a legacy of the year 1972, when the city hosted the Olympic Games. Bayern Munich, the city's soccer team and a frequent champion of the Bundesliga (National League), is a source of considerable civic pride. As is true of many of Germany's cities, Munich was damaged heavily by Allied bombing raids during World War II. For that reason, most of its buildings are modern, but its streets do boast some of the finest examples of baroque architecture to be found in Germany.

Work, Work, and Build Your Little House

Stuttgart is the most important city of Swabia, a region of the southwest federal republic that is part of the Land of Baden-Württemberg. Germans are often stereotyped as slavish adherents of the work ethic; to other Germans, Swabians are known for their devotion to hard work, frugality, their Protestant faith, and family. Work, work, and build your little house is the traditional Swabian motto. Home to Daimler-Benz (manufacturers of Mercedes Benz automobiles), the electronics conglomerate Bosch, Porsche automobiles, and the German headquarters of IBM, Stuttgart has been a leading creator and beneficiary of the economic miracle, yet its people, unlike the denizens of Munich, consider it extremely poor taste to demonstrate their wealth. It retains something of a pastoral quality; from this region comes much of Germany's wine, and many citizens, even within the city, maintain small plots on which they grow grapes and other fruits and vegetables. A good portion of the inner city has been declared a pedestrian zone—a somewhat ironic touch in the city where in 1883 Gottlieb Daimler invented the first vehicle to be propelled by an internal combustion engine and which remains Germany's center of high technology, yet indicative of the Swabian commitment to quality of life.

Mainhattan

Mainhattan is the name its critics have given Frankfurt, the city of about 625,000 people, located on the Main River, that will no doubt remain Germany's banking and financial center. The slur, as it is considered, is directed primarily at Frankfurt's architecture, for the city center has Europe's densest collection of skyscrapers, but it also pertains to Frankfurt's preoccupation with what Germans consider an American obsession—making money. Frankfurt became one of Germany's financial powers in the late 19th century, when it was home to many of the prominent Jewish families, including the Rothschilds, who served as the nation's most important financiers. Today it is the location of the German stock exchange, most of the country's leading banks, and dozens of financial services concerns, but its detractors overlook its myriad cultural attractions, including the Goethe Haus, birthplace and

Frankfurt, which was rebuilt after World War II, is Germany's financial center and is noted in Europe for its numerous skyscrapers. Goethe, who was born in Frankfurt, called the city the "secret capital" because of its prosperous and cosmopolitan nature.

home to the poet and playwright, and a magnificent cathedral, where from 1562 to 1806 the Habsburg Holy Roman Emperors were crowned. Two of Germany's most influential daily newspapers are published in the city, and each year the Frankfurt Book Fair attracts publishers from around the world.

Hamburg

A Free and Hanseatic City is the designation still proudly used by the north German city of Hamburg, a self-contained Land. Germany's busiest port and largest city, Hamburg is also the nation's media capital. Most of the television news programs are broadcast from Hamburg, and the leading weekly newsmagazines are published there. Like other West German cities of the north, Hamburg has suffered somewhat in recent years from the tendency of German industry to relocate in the south, but its economic base remains sound, and the tonnage unloaded at its docks increased by half in the early 1980s. One of the least pro-Nazi cities in Germany during the Hitler years, Hamburg has been a socialist stronghold since the late 19th century. Because it was virtually destroyed twice in one century—by fire in the mid-19th century and by Allied bombs during World War II—Hamburg is one of Germany's most modern cities in terms of architecture, but in rebuilding it was able to avoid much of the congestion that characterizes other German urban areas. As befits its location astride the Elbe and the North Sea, Hamburg remains the city of bridges— it boasts almost 2,200 of them, compared with some 400 in Venice, the Italian city famed for its marine setting. The birthplace of the great composers Felix Mendelssohn and Johannes Brahms, Hamburg maintains a proud cultural tradition, chiefly through the achievements of its opera house, which many observers regard as Germany's best.

Sharing the Wealth

One factor uniting all the regions of West Germany was that all had benefited from the sustained economic growth that was the most remarkable aspect of the history of West Germany. The West German economy was remarkably consistent. Even during the economic downturn that adversely affected most of the world economy in the late 1970s and early 1980s, the West German economy continued to grow, albeit at a slightly lower rate than in the past. At the time of reunification, West Germany's gross domestic product (GDP), the measure of newly available goods and services, was by far the highest in Europe, and its per capita gross national product trailed only those of the United States and Japan. The high quality of its manufactured goods had long kept West Germany one of the world's biggest exporters, and it had consistently maintained an extremely favorable balance of trade. For all its relative lack of economic achievement in comparison with its Western counterpart, East Germany maintained what was probably the eastern bloc's strongest economy; the union of the two Germanys immediately created the world's largest exporter and a nation second only to Japan in terms of favorable balance of trade. Industry and manufacturing continue to be the most important segments of the German economy, with trade and services almost as significant. Agriculture contributes only a very small amount to the GNP. Because West Germany was so densely populated and only one-third of the land was arable, most farms were extremely small, family-run affairs. In the 1970s, more than two-thirds of them were less than 25 acres in size—too small even to support a family.

Overall, the German economy has shown a remarkable ability to adapt to changing circumstances, from the immediate postwar period to the present. In the 1970s, the Ruhr area, Europe's most important coal-mining and steel production region, entered a period of decline not unlike that suffered by the so-called Rust Belt areas of the United States during that same period. Recognizing that changing energy and economic needs threatened to render its traditional economic base obsolete, the Ruhr has begun a transition to new industries—petrochemicals, automobile construction, and factories for the production of consumer goods. At the time of reunification, unemployment in all of West Germany continued to be remarkably low.

All this wealth has created a way of life that is in many aspects similar to that of Americans. Germans dress much as Americans do and like Americans, they have the luxury of choosing from an incredible variety of consumer items. The majority of Germans own televisions and cars. These automobiles have one of the most sophisticated highway systems in the world to ride on, and non-drivers can reach most major German cities by rail or airplane. Most German cities, but especially Hamburg and Munich, feature up-to-date public transportation systems. West Germany trailed only the United States in terms of rate of car ownership per citizen, and television was credited with playing a significant role in hastening reunification. Although in their daily life East Germans were forced to confront a bewildering array of government restrictions, they were able to watch news shows and other television programs from West Germany, which greatly increased their awareness of the disparity in the way of life in the two Germanys.

In early 1990, church membership was higher in West Germany than it was in the United States—96 percent of West Germans professed membership in the Protestant or Catholic faith and paid a government tax for their support—but actual participation in church services was comparatively low. Homes in Germany tend to be smaller than in the United States, and the majority of Germans live in apartments rather than in single-family houses. Despite regional differences, Germany has little of the ethnic diversity that characterizes American society. What racial animosity exists is directed at the guest workers, or Gastarbeiter, as the 4 million Turks, Yugoslavs, Iberians, and Greeks who were

Germany's autobahn, or expressway, system is well known for its design, intended predominantly for speed. The first stretch of the autobahn was opened in 1935 between Frankfurt and Darmstadt.

invited to West Germany to fill menial and lower-paying positions during the height of the Wirtschaftswunder are known. The greatest number of these—perhaps one-third—are Turks. For the most part, these guest workers live a sort of outcast existence and have never been fully integrated into German society.

Germany and the Future

In the past couple of decades, West Germany had been the only Western nation where the death rate had exceeded the birth rate. Indeed, if not for the steady flow of refugees it had received, the population of the Federal Republic of Germany would have declined during that period. The most common explanation for this phenomenon is that it reflects a profound uncertainty about the future on the part of the German people. Obviously, for the West Germans the horrors of their not so recent past still cast a long shadow over their considerable current achievements.

How will reunification affect this German *Angst*, or fear? It is, of course, impossible to predict with certainty, but some things seem likely. No longer will the Federal Republic of Germany be referred to alternately as West Germany; most likely it will remain the name for a new, unified German nation. The post–World War II period will be studied as merely one chapter in the long history of the German nation, like the Weimar years or the Bismarck era. In the immediate future, Germany's economic predominance in Europe will only increase; already, fears of German might have proved to be something of a stumbling block as concerns the final plans for the creation of the European Community.

And what of the fears possessed by many Europeans, and even some Germans, concerning the dangers of a resurgent, unified Germany? In the years since World War II, the West German educational system proved singularly adept at preparing its charges to fill the needs of the nation's economy. After four years of education at a primary school, called a *Grundschule*, at age 10 West

German students were funneled toward either academic or vocational training. The latter taught the student an employable skill or trade; at age 15 the student began serving a part-time apprenticeship in his or her chosen field. Those who received academic training generally stayed in school (called *Gymnasium*) until they were 18, at which time they were able to take the *Abitur*, an examination, successful completion of which virtually guaranteed them admission to university. From this class of students were drawn West Germany's professional and intellectual classes. This process had its drawbacks, most notably the perpetuation of a fairly rigid class system, but the concept of *Mitbestimmungsrecht*, or codetermination, the powerful position of West German labor unions, the high wages paid workers, and the German belief in cooperative as opposed to strictly individual initiative had all helped to alleviate the strains that might be expected to result. And there is no denying that a skilled, highly trained, motivated work force was the most significant West German resource.

Observers have been less united in their opinions on the success of the West German educational system in attaining its other primary goal—instilling democratic values by making young Germans aware of the mistakes of the past. Only time will tell how permanent the German commitment to democracy is. West Germany survived several serious challenges—the refugee problem, the ongoing cold war tension, the Berlin crisis of the early 1960s, a wave of leftist terrorism in the 1970s—without compromising its commitment to democratic principles. Judging by the consistently high voter turnout in national elections, West Germans were enthusiastic participants in their democratic experiment. Still, the greatest challenges lie ahead. Given such a turbulent past, skeptics about Germany's future can be forgiven their doubts; given so many remarkable German achievements, optimists must be allowed their hopes.

GLOSSARY

Aryan   Pre-Christian warlike tribe of nomads who overran much of Asia Minor and India. Hitler's racial propaganda ascribed the supposed racial superiority of the German people to their alleged descent from the Aryans. Such features as blue eyes and blond hair were characterized by Hitler as quintessentially and desirably Aryan.

Bundesrat   The upper house of the West German legislature.

Bundestag   The lower house of the West German legislature, consisting of the delegations from the *Länder*.

Bundeswehr   The army of the Federal Republic of Germany.

Carolingian Empire   The kingdom presided over by Charlemagne and his ancestors and descendants; at its greatest extent, it included present-day France and Germany.

cold war   The ideological, economic, and political struggle between the United States and its allies and the Soviet Union and its allies that took place during the 45 years following the end of World War II.

Führer German word meaning leader; the title assumed by Hitler.

Grundschule An elementary or primary school attended by West German children until the age of 10.

Hochdeutsch High German; the national language of public discourse in both East and West Germany.

Holy Roman Empire of the German Nation The unwieldy, loosely defined political entity conceived as a successor state to the Roman Empire. The Holy Roman Empire lasted from 962 to 1806; its head, who until the 16th century was crowned by the pope, was considered to be the temporal head of the Roman Catholic church as well as king of the Germans. In reality, however, the emperor and the pope often clashed; and the emperor, although claiming an often significant degree of loyalty from his German subjects, was never able to unite the many distinct German states.

investiture The right to select individuals to fill church offices. Disputes over investiture often divided the Holy Roman Emperor and the pope.

Kaiser German word meaning Caesar; analogous to the Russian word czar, it was the title assumed by Germany's emperors from 1871 to 1918.

Länder The German word for states; the 10 individual states that constitute the Federal Republic of Germany (West Germany).

Landtag The Prussian parliament; also the legislative assembly of a *Land*.

Mitbestimmungsrecht Codetermination; it refers to the cooperation of ownership, management, and labor in making decisions about the future course of individual economic institutions and the West German economy as a whole.

Ostpolitik Eastern policy; it refers to Chancellor Willy Brandt's policy of *rapprochement* (reconciliation) with East Germany.

Realpolitik The theory or exercise of politics based on practical rather than ethical or theoretical considerations; the practitioner of realpolitik, such as Bismarck, is likely to weigh national interest and power as more important than conventional conceptions of morality.

Reich German word meaning empire. There have been three reichs in German history: The Holy Roman Empire of the German Nation, which lasted from 962 to 1806; the German empire created by Bismarck in 1871, which lasted until 1918; and Hitler's self-proclaimed Third Reich, which lasted from 1933 to 1945.

Reichstag The lower house of the German parliament between 1871 and 1918.

Soziale Marktwirtschaft Socially responsive free-market economy; devised by Adenauer and Erhard, such an economy combines private ownership with active participation by the government.

Stunde Null The zero hour; used to refer to the immediate aftermath of Germany's defeat in World War II.

Wirtschaftswunder The "economic miracle" that transformed the West German economy from its ruinous condition following World War II to one of the world's strongest.

INDEX